MW00424653

"It is suddenly in fashion to decry global economy. But Michael Yates has been warning us about growing inequality for years, and explaining how it is not just an inconvenient side effect of poorly managed capitalism but rather part of its very core. Capitalism by definition is unjust. Once again Michael Yates provides a clear, timely, and powerful book explaining our economy, dissecting varieties of mainstream economic thought, and inspiring readers to fight for a more just world."

Stephanie Luce, Professor of Labor Studies, Murphy Institute/CUNY and Professor of Sociology, The Graduate Center CUNY

"One of the many things I've always admired about Michael Yates is his courage. Yates has the guts to go inside the belly of the beast and return with a tale as stark and immediate as Dante's descent into the Inferno. His vitally important book *The Great Inequality* is nothing less than a necropsy of the collateral damage inflicted by unfettered capitalism, detailing in vivid prose how a predatory economic system has wrecked communities, immiserated lives, looted the environment and subverted our democracy. But Yates never submits to fatalism. His book is an alarum for our attenuated times, piercing through the white noise of the media, calling us off our couches and onto the streets."

Jeffrey St. Clair, editor *CounterPunch*, author of *Born Under a Bad Sky*

"As economists and pundits make glib pronouncements about the inevitability, the immorality, or the paradox of inequality, Michael Yates lays bare the real source: capitalism. In crystal clear prose, he demonstrates that the system we are currently burdened with produces inequality in all realms of social life, resulting in a prolonged social death not only for the exploited class but for the planet as a whole. Read this book. Heed its warning. Our very survival may depend on it."

Robin D. G. Kelley, author of *Freedom Dreams: The Black Radical Imagination*

"This is another fine book by Michael Yates. *The Great Inequality* is an account of the roots of the momentous rising inequality we are witnessing today, which it describes as the 'consequence of uncontested employer power.' Yates' timely prescription is not so much focused on policy changes (although he discusses these aplenty) as it is on the need for a particular kind or orientation of action in solidarity: we need 'radical change, with black America in the lead.' Read this book if you want to understand the present and perhaps help change the future."

Eric Schutz, Professor Emeritus, Rollins College

The Great Inequality

A growing inequality in income and wealth marks modern capitalism, and it negatively affects nearly every aspect of our lives, especially those of the working class. It is and will continue to be the central issue of politics in almost every nation on earth. In this book, the author explains inequality in clear, passionate, and intelligent prose: what it is, why it matters, how it affects us, what its underlying causes are, and what we might do about it. This book was written to encourage informed radical action by working people, the unemployed, and the poor, uniquely blending the author's own experiences with his ability to make complex issues comprehensible to a mass audience. This book will be excellent for courses in a variety of disciplines, and it will be useful to activists and the general reading public.

Michael D. Yates is a writer, editor, and labor educator. He is currently associate editor of *Monthly Review* magazine and editorial director of Monthly Review Press. He served as professor of economics at University of Pittsburgh-Johnstown from 1969–2001 and adjunct professor of labor studies at UMass-Amherst from 1998–2014. He and his wife Karen Korenoski have been traveling the United States for the past fourteen years. These travels are recounted in his book *Cheap Motels and a Hot Plate: An Economist's Travelogue.*

Critical Interventions: Politics, Culture, and the Promise of Democracy
Edited by Henry A. Giroux, Susan Searls Giroux, and Kenneth J. Saltman

The Great Inequality

Michael D. Yates

Routledge
Taylor & Francis Group

NEW YORK AND LONDON

First published 2016
by Routledge
711 Third Avenue, New York, NY 10017

and by Routledge
2 Park Square, Milton Park, Abingdon, Oxon, OX14 4RN

Routledge is an imprint of the Taylor & Francis Group, an informa business

Library of Congress Cataloging in Publication Data
Yates, Michael, 1946– author.
  The great inequality/Michael D. Yates.
  pages cm.—(Critical interventions)
  1. Income distribution—United States. 2. Equality—United States.
  3. Wealth—United States. 4. Social classes—United States. 5. United
  States—Economic conditions—21st century. 6. United States—Social
  conditions—21st century. I. Title.
  HC110.I5Y37 2016
  339.2′20973—dc23
  2015029598

ISBN: 978-1-138-18344-5 (hbk)
ISBN: 978-1-138-18345-2 (pbk)
ISBN: 978-1-315-64584-1 (ebk)

Typeset in Adobe Caslon Pro, Copperplate and Trade Gothic
by Florence Production Ltd, Stoodleigh, Devon, UK

Printed and bound in the United States of America by
Edwards Brothers Malloy on sustainably sourced paper

To Karen, as always my strongest supporter, best critic, and constant companion

CONTENTS

ILLUSTRATIONS

Figures

Table

FOREWORD

American society is morally bankrupt and politically broken, and its vision of the future appears utterly dystopian. As the United States descends into the dark abyss of an updated form of totalitarianism, the unimaginable has become imaginable in that it has become possible not only to foresee the death of the essential principles of constitutional democracy, but also the birth of what Hannah Arendt once called the horror of dark times. The politics of terror, a culture of fear, and the spectacle of violence dominate America's cultural apparatuses and legitimate the ongoing militarization of public life and American society. Unchecked corporate power and a massive commodification, infantilization, and depoliticization of the polity have become the totalitarian benchmarks defining American society. In part, this is due to the emergence of a brutal modern-day capitalism, or what some might call neoliberalism. This form of neoliberal capitalism is a particularly savage, cruel, and exploitative regime of oppression in which not only are the social contract, civil liberties, and the commons under siege, but also the very notion of the political, if not the planet itself. The dystopian moment facing the United States, if not most of the globe, can be summed up in Fred Jameson's contention "that it is easier to imagine the end of the world than to imagine the end of capitalism." He goes on to say, "We can now revise that and witness the attempt to imagine capitalism by way of imagining the end of the world." One way of understanding Jameson's comment is through the ideological and affective spaces in which the neoliberal subject is produced and market-driven ideologies are normalized. Capitalism has made a virtue out of self-interest and the pursuit of material wealth and in doing so has created a culture of shattered dreams and a landscape filled with "Broken highways, bankrupt cities, collapsing bridges, failed schools, the unemployed, the underpaid and the uninsured: all suggest a collective failure of will. These shortcomings are so endemic that we no longer know how to talk about what is wrong, much less set about repairing it."[1]

Yet, there is a growing recognition that casino capitalism is driven by a kind of mad violence and form of self-sabotage and that if it does not come to an end what we will experience in all probability is the destruction of human life and the planet itself. Certainly, more recent scientific reports on the threat of ecological disaster from researchers at the University of Washington, NASA, and the Intergovernmental Panel on Climate Change reinforce this dystopian possibility. The under-mining of public trust and public values has now given way to a market-driven discourse that produces a society that has lost any sense of democratic vision and social purpose and in doing so resorts to state terrorism, the criminalization of social problems, and a culture of cruelty. Institutions that were once defined to protect and enhance human life now function largely to punish and maim.

As Michael Yates points out throughout this book, capitalism is devoid of any sense of social responsibility and is driven by an unchecked desire to accumulate capital at all costs. As power becomes global and politics remains local, ruling elites no longer make political conces-sions to workers or any other group that they either exploit or consider disposable. Security and crisis have become the new passwords for imposing a culture of fear and for imposing what Giorgio Agamben has called a permanent state of exception and a technology of government repression.[2] A constant appeal to a state of crisis becomes the new normal for arming the police, curtailing civil liberties, expanding the punishing state, criminalizing everyday behavior, and suppressing dissent. Fear now

drives the major narratives that define the United States and give rise
to dominant forms of power, free from any sense of moral and political
conviction, if not accountability. In the midst of this dystopian
nightmare, there is the deepening abyss of inequality, one that not only
separates the rich from the poor, but also increasingly relegates the
middle and working classes to the ranks of the precariat. Concentrations
of wealth and income generate power for the financial elite and
unchecked misery for most people, a fear/insecurity industry, and a
growing number of social pathologies.

Michael Yates in *The Great Inequality* provides a road map for both
understanding the registers that produce inequality as well as the
magnitude of the problems it poses across a range of commanding
spheres extending from health care and the political realm to the
environment and education. At the same time, he exposes the myths
that buttress the ideology of inequality. These include an unchecked
belief in boundless economic growth, the notion that inequality is
chosen freely by individuals in the market place, and the assumption
that consumption is the road to happiness. Unlike a range of recent books
on inequality, Yates goes beyond exposing the mechanisms that drive
inequality and the panoply of commanding institutions that support it.
He also provides a number of strategies that challenge the deep
concentrations of wealth and power while delivering a number of
formative proposals that are crucial for nurturing a radical imagination
and the social movements necessary to struggle for a society that no
longer equates capitalism with democracy.

As Yates makes clear throughout this book, money now engulfs
everything in this new age of disposability. Moreover, when coupled
with a weakening of movements to counter the generated power of
capitalists, the result has been a startling increase in the influence
of predatory capitalism, along with inequities in wealth, income, power,
and opportunity. Such power breeds more than anti-democratic
tendencies, it also imposes constraints, rules, and prohibitions on the
99 percent whose choices are increasingly limited to merely trying to
survive. Capitalists are no longer willing to compromise and have
expanded their use of power to dominate economic, political, and social

life. For Yates, it is all the more crucial to understand how power works under the reign of global capitalism in order to grasp the magnitude of inequality, the myriad of factors that produce it, and what might be done to change it.

Accompanying the rise of a savage form of capitalism and the ever-expanding security state is the emergence of new technologies and spaces of control. One consequence is that labor power is increasingly produced by machines and robotic technologies which serve to create "a large pool of more or less unemployed people." Moreover, as new technologies produce massive pools of unused labor, it also is being used as a repressive tool for collecting "unlimited biometric and genetic information of all of its citizens."[3] The ongoing attack on the working class is matched by new measures of repression and surveillance. This new weaponized face of capitalism is particularly ominous given the rise of the punishing state and the transformation of the United States from a democracy in progress to a fully developed authoritarian society. Every act of protest is now tainted, labeled by the government and mainstream media as either treasonous or viewed as a potential act of terrorism. For example, animal rights activists are put on the terrorist list. Whistle-blowers such as Edward Snowden are painted as traitors. Members of the Black Lives Matter movement are put under surveillance,[4] all electronic communication is now subject to government spying, and academics who criticize government policy are denied tenure or worse.

Under neoliberalism, public space is increasingly converted into private space undermining those spheres necessary for developing a viable sense of social responsibility, while also serving to transform citizenship into mostly an act of consumption. Under such circumstances, the notion of crisis is used both to legitimate a system of economic terrorism as well as to accentuate an increasing process of depoliticization. Within this fog of market induced paralysis, language is subject to the laws of capitalism, reduced to a commodity, and subject to the "tyranny of the moment . . . emaciated, impoverished, vulgarized and squeezed out of the meanings it was resumed to carry."[5]

As the latest stage of predatory capitalism, neoliberalism is part of a broader economic and political project of restoring class power and consolidating the rapid concentration of capital, particularly financial capital.[6] As a political project it includes "the deregulation of finance, privatization of public services, elimination and curtailment of social welfare programs, open attacks on unions, and routine violations of labor laws."[7] As an ideology, it casts all dimensions of life in terms of market rationality, construes profit making as the arbiter and essence of democracy, consuming as the only operable form of citizenship, and upholds the irrational belief that the market can both solve all problems and serve as a model for structuring all social relations. As a mode of governance, it produces identities, subjects, and ways of life driven by a survival-of-the-fittest ethic, grounded in the idea of the free, possessive individual, and committed to the right of ruling groups and institutions to exercise power removed from matters of ethics and social costs. As a policy and political project, it is wedded to the privatization of public services, the dismantling of the connection of private issues and public problems, the selling off of state functions, liberalization of trade in goods and capital investment, the eradication of government regulation of financial institutions and corporations, the destruction of the welfare state and unions, and the endless marketization and commodification of society.

Nothing engenders the wrath of conservatives more than the existence of the government providing a universal safety net, especially one that works, such as either Medicare or Social Security. As Yates points out, government is viewed by capitalists as an institution that gets in the way of capital. One result is a weakening of social programs and provisions. As Paul Krugman observes regarding the ongoing conservative attacks on Medicare, "The real reason conservatives want to do away with Medicare has always been political: It's the very idea of the government providing a universal safety net that they hate, and they hate it even more when such programs are successful."[8] In opposition to Krugman and other liberal economists, Michael Yates argues rightly in this book that the issue is not simply preserving Medicare but eliminating the predatory system that disavows equality of wealth, power, opportunity, and health care for everyone.

Neoliberalism has put an enormous effort into creating a commanding cultural apparatus and public pedagogy in which individuals can only view themselves as consumers, embrace freedom as the right to participate in the market, and supplant issues of social responsibility for an unchecked embrace of individualism and the belief that all social relations be judged according to how they further one's individual needs and self-interests. Matters of mutual caring, respect, and compassion for the other have given way to the limiting orbits of privatization and unrestrained self-interest, just as it has become increasingly difficult to translate private troubles into larger social, economic, and political considerations. One consequence is that it has become more difficult for people to debate and question neoliberal hegemony and the widespread misery it produces for young people, the poor, middle class, workers, and other segments of society—now considered disposable under neoliberal regimes which are governed by a survival-of-the-fittest ethos, largely imposed by the ruling economic and political elite. Unable to make their voices heard and lacking any viable representation in the process makes clear the degree to which the American public, in particular, are suffering under a democratic deficit producing a profound dissatisfaction that does not always translate into an understanding of how neoliberal capitalism has destroyed democracy or what it might mean to understand and challenge its diverse apparatuses of persuasion and power. Clearly, the surge of popularity behind the presidential candidacy of a buffoon such as Donald Trump testifies to both a deep seated desire for change and the forms it can take when emotion replaces reason and any viable analysis of capitalism and its effects seem to be absent from a popular sensibility.

What Michael Yates makes clear in this incisive book on inequality is that democratic values, commitments, integrity, and struggles are under assault from a wide range of sites in an age of intensified violence and disposability. Throughout the book he weaves a set of narratives and critiques in which he lays bare the anti-democratic tendencies that are on display in a growing age of lawlessness and disposability. He not only makes clear that inequality is not good for the economy, social bonds, the environment, politics, and democracy, Yates also argues that capitalism in the current historical moment is marked by an age that thrives on racism, xenophobia, the purported existence of an alleged culture of criminality, and a massive system of inequality that affects all aspects of society. Worth repeating is that at the center of this book, unlike so many others tackling inequality, is an attempt to map a number of modalities that give shape and purpose to widespread disparities in wealth and income, including the underlying forces behind inequality, how it works to secure class power, how it undermines almost every viable foundation needed for a sustainable democracy, and what it might mean to develop a plan of action to produce the radical imagination and corresponding modes of agency and practice that can think and act outside of the reformist politics of capitalism.

Unlike so many other economists, such as Paul Krugman and Joseph Stiglitz who address the issue of inequality, Yates refuses the argument that the system is simply out of whack and can be fixed. Nor does he believe that capitalism can be described only in terms of economic structures. Capitalism is both a symbolic pathological economy that produces particular dispositions, values, and identities as well as oppressive institutional apparatuses and economic structures. Yates goes even further arguing that capitalism is not only about authoritarian ideologies and structures, it is also about the crisis of ideas, agency, and the failure of people to react to the suffering of others and to the conditions of their own oppression. Neoliberal capitalism has no language for human suffering, moral evaluation, and social responsibility. Instead, it creates a survival-of-the-fittest ethos buttressed by a discourse that is morally insensitive, sadistic, cannibalistic, and displays a hatred of those whose labor cannot be exploited, do not buy into the consumerist ethic, or are considered other by virtue of their race, class, and ethnicity. Neoliberalism is the discourse of shadow games, committed to highlighting corporate power and making invisible the suffering of others, all the while leaving those considered disposable in the dark to fend for themselves.

Yates makes visible not only the economic constraints that bear down on the poor and disposable in the neoliberal age of precarity, he also narrates the voices, conditions, hardships, and suffering workers have to endure in a variety of occupations ranging from automobile workers and cruise ship workers to those who work in restaurants and as harvesters on farms. He provides a number of invaluable statistics that chart the injuries of class and race under capitalism but rather than tell a story with only statistics and mind-boggling data, he also provides stories that give flesh to the statistics that mark a new historical conjuncture and a wide range of hardships that render work for most people hell and produce what has been called the hidden injuries of class. Much of what he writes is informed by a decade-long research trip across the United States in which he attempted to see first-hand what the effects of capitalism have been on peoples' lives, the environment, work, unions, and other crucial spheres that inform everyday life. His keen eye is particularly riveting as he describes his teaming up with Cesar Chavez and the United Farm Workers in the 1970s and his growing disappointment with a union that increasingly betrayed its own principles.

For Yates, the capitalist system is corrupt, malicious, and needs to be replaced. Capitalism leaves no room for the language of justice, the social, or, for that matter, democracy itself. In fact, one of its major attributes is to hide its effects of power, racial injustice, militarized state violence, domestic terrorism, and new forms of disposability, especially regarding those marginalized by class and race. The grotesque inequalities produced by capitalism are too powerful, deeply rooted in the social and economic fabric, and unamenable to liberal reforms. Class disparities constitute a machinery of social death, a kind of zombie-like machine that drains life out of most of the population poisoning both existing and future generations.

The politics of disposability has gone mainstream as more and more individuals and groups are now considered surplus and vulnerable, consigned to zones of abandonment, surveillance, and incarceration. At one level, the expansive politics of disposability can be seen in the rising numbers of homeless, the growing army of debt-ridden students, the increasingly harsh treatment of immigrants, the racism that fuels the school-to-prison pipeline, and the growing attack on public servants. On another level, the politics of disposability has produced a culture of lawlessness and cruelty evident by the increasing rollback of voting rights, the war waged against women's reproductive rights, laws that discriminate against gays, the rise of the surveillance state, and the growing militarization of local police forces. Yates argues convincingly that there is a desperate need for a new language for politics, solidarity, shared responsibilities, and democracy itself. Yates sees in the now largely departed Occupy Movement an example of a movement that used a new discourse and set of slogans to highlight inequality, make class inequities visible, and to showcase the workings of power in the hands of the financial elite. For Yates, Occupy provided a strategy that can be and is being emulated by a number of groups, especially those emerging in the black community in opposition to police violence. Such a strategy begins by asking what a real democracy looks like and how does it compare to the current society in which we live. One precondition for individual and social agency is that the horizons for change must transcend the parameters of the existing society, and the future must be configured in such a way as to not mimic the present.

What is remarkable about *The Great Inequality* is that Yates does not simply provide a critique of capitalism in its old and new forms, he also provides a discourse of possibility developed around a number of suggested policies and practices designed to not reform capitalism but to abolish it. This is a book that follows in the manner of Dr. Martin Luther King's call to break the silence. In it Yates functions as a moral witness in reporting on the hardships and suffering produced by grotesque forms of inequality. As such, he reveals the dark threats that capitalism in its ruthlessly updated versions poses to the planet. Yet, his narrative is never far from either hope or a sense that there is a larger public for whom his testimony matters and that such a public is capable of collective resistance. *The Great Inequality* also serves to enliven the ethical imagination, and speak out for those populations now considered outcast and voiceless. Yates provides a furious reading of inequality and the larger structure of capitalism. In doing so he exhibits a keen and incisive intellect along with a welcomed sense of righteous fury.

Henry A. Giroux
McMaster University

Notes

1   Tony Judt, Ill Fares the Land (New York, N.Y.: The Penguin Press, 2010), 12.
2   Giorgio Agamben, "The Security State and a Theory of Destituent Power," Philosophers for Change, (February 25, 2014). Online: http://philosophersforchange.org/2014/02/25/the-security-state-and-a-theory-of-destituent-power/
3   Ibid., Agamben, "The Security State and a Theory of Destituent Power."
4   George Joseph, "Exclusive: Feds regularly monitored black lives matter since Ferguson," Intercept (July 24, 2015). Online: https://firstlook.org/theintercept/2015/07/24/documents-show-department-homeland-security-monitoring-black-lives-matter-since-ferguson/; Deirdre Fulton, "Exposed: Big Brother Targets Black Lives: Government spying can be an 'effective way to chill protest movements,' warns Center for Constitutional Rights," CommonDreams (July 24, 2015). Online: http://commondreams.org/news/2015/07/24/exposed-big-brother-targets-black-lives
5   Zygmunt Bauman and Leonidas Donskis, Moral Blindness: The Loss of Sensitivity in Liquid Modernity (Cambridge, U.K.: Polity Press, 2013), 46.
6   I have taken up the issue of neoliberalism extensively in Henry A. Giroux, Against the Terror of Neoliberalism (Boulder: Paradigm, 2008). See also, David Harvey, A Brief History of Neoliberalism (New York: Oxford University Press, 2007); Manfred B. Steger and Ravi K. Roy, Neoliberalism: A Very Short Introduction (New York: Oxford University Press, 2010); Gerard Dumenil and Dominique Levy, The Crisis of Neoliberalism (Cambridge: Harvard University Press, 2011). Henry A. Giroux, Twilight of the Social (Boulder: Paradigm, 2013); Henry A. Giroux, Against the Violence of Organized Forgetting: Beyond America's Disimagination Machine (San Francisco: City Lights, 2014); Wendy Brown, Undoing the Demos: Neoliberalism's Stealth Revolution (Cambridge: Zone Books 2015).
7   Michael D. Yates, "Occupy Wall Street and the Significance of Political Slogans," Counterpunch, (February 27, 2013). Online: http://counterpunch.org/2013/02/27/occupy-wall-street-and-the-significance-of-political-slogans/
8   Paul Krugman, "Zombies Against Medicare," New York Times (July 27, 2015). Online: http://nytimes.com/2015/07/27/opinion/zombies-against-medicare.html?_r=0

ACKNOWLEDGMENTS

Henry Giroux was instrumental in getting this book published. For this, his helpful suggestions, and for his steadfast support, I thank him. Thanks, too, to Dean Birkenkamp for his gracious encouragement.

Most of these chapters have appeared in different versions in various magazines. I have thoroughly edited, updated, and provided end notes for them:

"The Great Inequality," first appeared in *Monthly Review*, 63/10 (March 2012).

"All the Economics You Need to Know in One Lesson," first appeared in *MRZine*, October 14, 2006.

"Markets Are the Problem, Not the Solution," first appeared in *Truthout*, April 16, 2014.

"Work Is Hell," first appeared in *CounterPunch*, May 20, 2009.

"The Injuries of Class," first appeared in *Monthly Review*, 59/8 (January 2008).

"It's Still Slavery by Another Name," is an amalgam of two essays: "It's Still Slavery by Another Name," which first appeared in *cheapmotelsandahotplate*, February 23, 2012 and "Black America and A New Freedom Budget" (co-authored with Paul Le Blanc), which first appeared in *Truthout*, September 12, 2013.

"The Ghosts of Karl Marx and Edward Abbey," first appeared in *Monthly Review*, 56/10 (March 2005).

"Cesar," first appeared in Michael D. Yates, *In and Out of the Working Class* (Winnipeg: ARP Books, 2009). Note that this is a work of creative nonfiction, and some names have been changed.

"OWS and the Importance of Political Slogans," first appeared in *cheapmotelsandahotplate*, February 28, 2013.

"The Growing Degradation of Work and Life and What We Might Do To End It," first appeared in *Truthout*, March 21, 2015.

1
INEQUALITY CASTS
A LONG SHADOW

A new park will soon be constructed along the shore of the Hudson River in Manhattan. Financed in large part by the billionaire couple Barry Diller and Diane von Furstenberg, who will contribute $130 million, it will be built on stilts above the water. It will feature "amphitheaters, footpaths, gardens," a perfect place, Ms. Furstensberg said to "rest, watch a sunset or performance."[1] Given that the park is adjacent to a gentrifying neighborhood, with sky-high rents, expensive restaurants, and hordes of well-heeled tourists, we can reasonably assume that not many poor city residents will use it for family outings or exercise. It will be one more haven for those at the top of the income and wealth distributions in a city that has become a playground for the super-rich, with one of the largest gaps in the nation between its most and least prosperous citizens. Meanwhile, parks in poorer areas languish from neglect. No wealthy donors revitalize either these or the neighborhoods surrounding them.[2]

The Diller-Furstenberg park is not an anomaly in New York City or in the country as a whole. Central Park is now maintained and aggrandized largely with private money, managed by a private nonprofit organization. Philadelphia, Tulsa, Houston, Pittsburgh, are all reliant on the largesse of the 1 percent for parks and the development of public spaces.[3] These are just one more example of the growing tendency in the United States and in most capitalist countries to privatize what were once public functions, subject at least minimally to democratic control. Public officials at all levels of government almost universally have applauded this development, pointing out that the strain on public finances has never been greater. They say that there is not enough money to pay for a host of what used to be public services, everything from parks to schools to hospitals. So we have no choice but to depend upon the generosity of those with the cash, and we should be grateful that they and their allies—Bill Gates and his billionaire brethren—are so civic-minded. Where would we be without them? Just as we would have missed out on all those great libraries without the philanthropy of Andrew Carnegie, we won't have places to play, good healthcare, or decent schools without the munificence of today's tycoons.

When I was a college teacher, I began to tell my students in the early 1980s that we were witnessing the beginning of a rise in inequality not seen since the 1920s. Every year I would show them charts illustrating the change in the distributions of income and wealth. The share of income going to the top 5 percent of income recipients grew nearly every year, and the wealth share grew steadily as well. I explained how the two distributions interacted to further increase inequality. A household with high income—the yearly sum of its wages, salaries, bonuses, dividends, interest, rents, profits from unincorporated businesses, and government transfer payments such as social security and subsidies to farmers—probably could not spend all of it. The remainder, the household's savings, would be used to purchase assets, such as stocks, bonds, real estate, precious metals, and works of art. These assets are what we mean by wealth. Most of them will generate income, either in the form of regular payments like dividends from stock or as capital gains when assets are sold at a price higher than that at which they were purchased. In this way, the household's income grows just because its wealth has risen. Those with low incomes will not be able to acquire assets and will not see their wealth rise. The more unequal incomes, the more unequal wealth will become.

If we begin with wealth, we get the same result. The Diller-von Furstenberg household has wealth of about $3.5 billion.[4] Let's suppose that the assets comprising their wealth yield a yearly return of 5 percent.

Their household income will rise by $175 million simply because they own income-producing possessions. If we add this income to their yearly salaries and bonuses, we see that their total income is enormous. They won't spend all of it, and therefore their wealth will grow. And on and on it will go. The rich will get richer, and the separation of them from the rest of us will widen. This will have nothing to do with how productive people are or what their contributions to society might be. I used to give my students an example of what I mean here. At one time Bill Gates had wealth of about $100 billion. Ignoring for the moment how he came to hold so much treasure, and assuming that he too received a 5 percent return, what would happen to his yearly income from his wealth if he were suddenly to go into a coma. He would continue to collect $5 billion year in and year out with no effort at all. No one can spend this much money every year, not even the most profligate of his caretakers, so Gates' wealth would automatically expand. Those without wealth will get no income from it, and again the gap between rich and poor becomes larger.

What is more, inequality will be maintained across generations. My parents died with almost no assets. What little there was had to be split five ways, giving but a tiny boost to my wealth and almost none to my future income. I was retired when my mother died, but had I been working, I could not have quit because my inheritance was large. Bill and Melinda Gates' children, on the other hand, will get such an enormous inheritance that they will never have to work again, and they will find that their wealth grows almost no matter what they do.

As we shall see throughout this book, mainstream economists have long served as apologists for rising inequality, either downplaying its severity or denying that it has adverse social consequences. One ingenious device is the concept of "human capital," first developed in the 1960s.[5] Working people could raise their productivity and their wages, with the latter depending on the former, by "investing" in themselves, mainly by securing more schooling and training. When they did this, they would increase their human capital. This reasoning implies that laborers and capitalists do the same thing. Workers buy additions to their human capital and get a return in the form of higher earnings.

Capitalists buy more capital, in the form of financial instruments that give them ownership of various kinds of property, and they get a return in the form of dividends, rent, interest, and profits. Both groups are in reality capitalists.

Unfortunately for the economists' theorizing, the analog breaks down because of a simple fact. Real property can be alienated from its owner, through a sale in the marketplace. Human capital cannot be separated from its owners; they must go with it because it is embodied in them. And when they die, their human capital perishes too. It cannot be willed to the children of those who made the investment. Given that most workers have little or no property, their offspring will have to work, just as their parents did. The more wealth accruing to a small minority, the greater the divide between workers and capitalists will be. Not only will the gap between rich and poor households grow, but that between the two great classes of persons in capitalist society will increase as well.

Once I provided my students with the data on income and wealth distribution and showed them how inequality had widened and once it did, why it would continue to increase, I made a prediction. I said that inequality would be the future's most important political issue. A good case can be made that I was right. The Occupy movement, the Arab Spring, the revolt in Syria against the Assad government, protests in Turkey, the burgeoning labor movement in China, the rise of Syriza in Greece have all been rooted in the unconscionable divide between the haves and have nots. And surely the incredible success of a 696-page, complex economic analysis of inequality, Thomas Piketty's *Capital in the Twenty-First Century*, indicates that this subject has come of age.[6] Given that, as shall become evident in Chapter 2, the conditions that gave rise to the "Great Inequality" have not abated and are, in fact, growing stronger, there is no doubt that inequality will inform all politics for the foreseeable future. If this is true, then an interrogation of inequality, in all of its many dimensions, will serve a useful purpose, informing readers and providing them with some ideas as to how we can create a more egalitarian society.

Before we sketch the consequences and causes of inequality, let us consider the view of most neoclassical (mainstream) economists that inequality does not matter. Harvard professor Martin Feldstein, who served under President Ronald Reagan as chairman of the Council of Economic Advisors, said in 2001, "Why there has been increasing inequality in this country is one of the big puzzles in our field and has absorbed a lot of intellectual effort." But he was unconcerned, suggesting that the effort has been wasted. "But if you ask me whether we should worry about the fact that some people on Wall Street and basketball players are making a lot of money, I say no."[7]

Economists like Feldstein conceptualize the economy as consisting of independent individuals who, faced with certain constraints, make decisions aimed at maximizing their well-being. Those who want higher incomes and wealth will make the appropriate investments in their human capital, and the increased productivity that results will automatically, through the market forces of demand and supply, raise their incomes. Then, if they choose to save some of this income, their wealth will grow as well. Those who fail to make human capital investments or to save their money will naturally fall behind those who do the opposite. Everything is a matter of choice, meaning that inequality is chosen by the participants in the marketplace. Some economists admit that the constraints people face are themselves unequal, but in this case, we must vote to elect officials who will enact public policies that remove such impediments to improvement.

Economists further argue that inequality is a socially good thing. They take the view of my paternal grandfather, an ardent conservative, who asked what incentive would there be for anyone to improve himself if we all had the same incomes. For him, as for the economists, human wants are unlimited, and we are all striving mightily, day and night, to satisfy as many of these insatiable desires as possible. We need incentives to work hard to do so, however, and what would be the point of working if everyone's incomes were equal. Inequality keeps our noses to the grindstone. What is more, our efforts to improve our own circumstances benefit society as a whole by augmenting the nation's aggregate output of goods and services, as well as the national income. A growing economy offers the only hope for the political alleviation of problems that the market cannot solve, even inequality itself, should it get so high that those at the bottom are demoralized. A stagnant economy, on the other hand, is bad for all of us. To put this another way, whatever individual and social difficulties inequality might entail, these are outweighed by the deleterious personal and societal impact of the low economic growth guaranteed by focusing too much on equality.

While this book examines the causes and consequences of inequality, it is also a sustained attack on the mainstream analysis of inequality, both its theory and its conclusions about inequality's consequences.[8] The chapters to follow afford detailed treatments, so here let me offer some prefatory remarks. First, inequality has little to do with individual choice or work incentives. If you are born into a poor family, you will inherit nothing; if your parents are rich, you very likely will be too. Your choices have nothing to do with this. And neoclassical economists seldom give much attention to the constraints we face and the fact that neither can these be overcome for most of us nor can public policies equalize them. If I have to borrow money to attend college and you do not, you will have a great advantage in terms of earning a high wage and accumulating wealth. I may not go to school if I have to borrow, and within the mainstream framework, this might be a rational choice. If the government provides me with a scholarship, this will not count for much if your parents' wealth has won them important connections that you can use to your labor market advantage. As for work incentives, we only have to look at past time periods in the United States or compare the United States to other countries to see that lower levels of inequality have neither made us lazier nor reduced the rate of economic growth.[9]

Inequality has its roots in unequal power. Those with more assets have more power than those who do not; that is, they can compel us to do what we would be unlikely to do otherwise. Here I do not mean the power of any particular person, although in a specific circumstance, this might be important. Critical is what is best-called class power. Most of us must work for wages to live. If we do not have employment, our lives will be difficult in every imaginable way, as anyone who has suffered an extended bout of unemployment knows. Unfortunately, we do not control our access to employment; we are at the mercy of our employers.

They have power over us, and there are many things we might do at their command rather than lose our jobs. We might accept pay cuts, work long hours, tolerate irregular shifts, endure unhealthy working conditions, and worse. Our employers are, for the most part, those who have the lion's share of society's assets and sit on the highest steps of the income and wealth ladders. Their power depends on our lack of wealth, so they will use theirs to exert control over us. As we will see, their wealth and income depends on our labor. But these things are embedded in the business entities they own. It is through these, through the corporations and other businesses that employ us, that the wealthy exert power. They work ceaselessly to organize businesses in such a way that their workers cannot easily wield a countervailing power. Even if employees organize together to confront their bosses, they will be confronted by the reality that employers have wealth enough to outlast them in any struggle. If they manage to defeat their adversary in a battle, they sooner or later will become victims of managerial control, replaced by machines or workers in another country when plants are closed and work is outsourced. In this way, a reserve army of labor is created and continuously replenished—enlarged greatly whenever the economy is struck by the recessions and depressions that have plagued capitalist economies almost from their birth—threatening those who have jobs with competition for the ability to earn a living.

There is an entire panoply of institutions that buttress the power and hence the monetary resources of the 1 percent. These include the government, the legal system, the media, the schools, and religion. All of these combine to form a culture and a way of looking at the world, what we might call an ideology, that tells us that what we have is good, that our society is the best on earth, the apex of human creation. That the inequality to which these institutions and the market system connected to them is either necessary or nothing to worry about. Occasionally we might have to make a few minor improvements to ensure that inequality doesn't get out of hand, but no radical departures are necessary. I will have a good deal to say about these institutions, but here allow me to make a second initial comment. Inequality and increases in it worsen a wide range of social outcomes.

Mainstream economists generally concern themselves with matters that can be quantified in money terms. Inequality is therefore thought to be simply a matter of money disparities among individuals or between various groups. They think of the negative consequences of it in terms of the opportunity of the participants in the marketplace to advance themselves materially, which ordinarily means the ability to consume more goods and services. This is usually summed up in the idea of equality of opportunity. They do not favor equality of outcome, only everyone having the same chance to make money. Severe inequality, which is never defined, is said to prevent equal opportunity, and it might be necessary for the government to pursue policies that "level the playing field." At root, this is an ideological argument, because these economists seldom argue that serious social costs will follow upon a significant economic distance between rich and poor. Rather, the poor might become disillusioned with the system and refuse to participate in it.

These economists, especially those with a liberal, Keynesian per-spective, say that inequality can slow down economic growth. This occurs because, as we know from empirical observation, the lower our income, the larger the fraction of it we spend. If income is shifted from poor to rich, the decline in spending by the poor will outweigh the increase in consumption by the wealthy. Therefore, the more unequal income becomes, other things equal, the smaller will be aggregate spending in the economy. That is, the lower will be consumer spending and the employment that depends upon it. To counter this, liberal economists recommend raising taxes on high incomes, increasing the minimum wage, making the earned income tax credit more generous, and increasing government spending. These would boost total spending and employment, because, for example, the taxes on the wealthy will be paid out of savings and therefore not reduce demand. But when the government spends the new tax revenues, overall demand, income, and employment will rise.

This effect of inequality is real, but it does not begin to grasp the impact inequality has on life in capitalist societies. The following briefly annotated list will give readers a preliminary grasp of the far-reaching consequences of an inequality now greater than at any time since the 1920s.

Politics

A nation with significant and growing inequality cannot be a democracy. The authors of a recent empirical study wrote:

> The central point that emerges from our research is that economic elites and organized groups representing business interests have substantial independent impacts on U.S. government policy, while mass-based interest groups and average citizens have little or no independent influence.[10]

Money calls the tune in U.S. politics. Hundreds of millions of dollars are spent every four years by presidential candidates, and it takes millions of dollars to run a successful congressional campaign. "A network of conservative advocacy groups backed by [multibillionaire brothers] Charles and David Koch aims to spend a staggering $889 million in advance of the next [2016] White House election, part of an expansive strategy to build on its 2014 victories that may involve jumping into the Republican primaries."[11] Getting access to this cash necessitates a close relationship between almost all persons seeking high political office and potential wealthy donors, as well as cash-rich corporations. *Quid pro quos* are always part of the bargain. From this flows a harsh conclusion. It is now nearly impossible to either get a man or woman dedicated to popular democracy elected or to secure passage of progressive legislation. What chance would an office-seeker dedicated to a robust expansion of social security, universal publicly-funded healthcare, better labor laws, sustainable, publicly-subsidized small-scale organic farming, and an end to fracking and other environmentally calamitous practices have of winning an election? Candidates are thoroughly vetted before any money is forthcoming. "Troublemakers" are eliminated from the start. Many political and business leaders expressed great interest in Piketty's book, but none have done anything to put into practice policies that would substantially reduce inequality. Nor are they likely to do so. What they have done and will continue to do is enact laws that enhance the already tremendous power of U.S. "oligarchs," those captains of finance who now rule the economy, and this, in turn, will put still more money in their pockets.

If we look at what governments do, who advises political leaders, who serves in appointed positions and on commissions, what politicians do after they leave office, who suffers when governments enact austerity measures, the conclusion is the same. The state is of, by, and for the wealthy. If I were to say that there are no longer any tribunes of the people, I would be exaggerating only slightly.[12]

Health

More so than any other developed capitalist country, good health care in the United States depends upon our ability to pay for it. Given this, it is no surprise that the lower your income, the worse are your physical and mental health.[13] And as income and wealth become more uneven, the demand for health care, and thus eventually its supply (higher demand increases profits, which call forth more supply), will tilt good health care provision toward the rich. They will get the best care, and most of the rest of us will get the worst. Their life expectancies will rise and their infant mortality rates fall; the opposite will occur for those who are poor. What is more, there is a substantial body of research that strongly suggests that inequality in and of itself affects health. If we compare two states with roughly the same average income, health will be worse in the state where income disparity is greatest. Falling further behind those above demoralizes us, generating stress and the accompanying poorer health that stress creates.[14] There is even some evidence now that the lack of income and inequality can harm those who are poor or discriminated against at the level of their DNA. "The urban poor in the United States are experiencing accelerated aging at the cellular level, and chronic stress linked both to income level and racial-ethnic identity is driving this physiological deterioration."[15]

There is also an interaction between the political oligarchy discussed above and health care, a connection that holds true for all of the other effects of inequality. Government healthcare policy will be largely determined by the needs of corporate America and the moneyed individuals who control it. National healthcare is held hostage to the private economy. Obamacare, for example, was put in place largely to guarantee gigantic cash flows to insurance and pharmaceutical companies. Whatever benefits it might offer to some poorer individuals were a secondary consideration.[16]

Education

What is true for health is true for schooling. Inequality gives rise to a two- or even three-tier system of education: elite private and a few superior public schools at one end, mediocre public and private (mainly religious) schools in the middle, and rundown second-rate public schools at the other, especially for racial minorities. As with healthcare, public education policy is steered into narrow channels of reforms that put money in the pockets of those who already have more than enough of it. Schools are now set up not for liberal education but to provide employers with cheap, pliable labor. For example, under No Child Left Behind and Race to the Top, classrooms have been restructured to resemble workplaces:

> Today urban schools are adroitly organized around the same principles as factory production lines. According to [Jonathan] Kozol, "raising test scores," "social promotion," "outcome-based objectives," "time management," "success for all," "authentic writing," "accountable talk," "active listening," and "zero noise" constitute part of the dominant discourse in public schools. Most urban public schools have adopted business and market "work related themes" and managerial concepts that have become part of the vocabulary used in classroom lessons and instruction. In the "market-driven classrooms," students "negotiate," "sign contracts," and take "ownership" of their own learning. In many classrooms, students can volunteer as the "pencil manager," "soap manager," "door manager," "line manager," "time manager," and "coat room manager." In some fourth-grade classrooms, teachers record student assignments and homework using "earning charts." In these schools,

teachers are referred to as "classroom managers," principals are identified as "building managers," and students are viewed as "learning managers." It is commonplace to view schoolchildren as "assets," "investment," "productive units," or "team players." Schools identify the skills and knowledge that students need to learn and acquire as "commodities" and the "products" to be consumed in the "educational marketplace." Under the current climate of the No Child Left Behind school reform movement, teachers are regarded as "efficiency technicians" and encouraged to use "strict Skinnerian control" methods and techniques to manage and teach students in their classroom. Kozol writes that in the market-driven model of public education, teachers are viewed as "floor managers" in public schools, "whose job it is to pump some 'added-value' into undervalued children."[17]

Today, wealthy private foundations and individuals have declared war on public schools, teachers, and especially teachers' unions. In league with the federal government, "the Gates Foundation, the Walton Foundation, the Broad Foundation, and the Dell Foundation, together with the Business Roundtable, education-industry organizations, like Pearson and McGraw-Hill, and the National Governors Association and the Council of Chief State School Officers"[18] are dismantling public schools and transforming them into adjuncts of private capital. Schools have always been purveyors of system-reinforcing ideology, but the schools of the future will be much more blatantly so. As inequality widens, capital will need ever-greater control of society if it is to prevent outright rebellion.

The lengths to which those seeking to kill critical education will go is illustrated by the jail terms meted out to several teachers, all African Americans, in Atlanta for altering answer sheets and giving students answers on standardized tests. The school district was run by a person gung-ho to raise scores on the examinations, and who had chastised and punished teachers who had protested the use of the tests. Then, teachers, fearful of losing their jobs if low test scores caused schools to be closed, taken over by the state, or privatized, did what many people do under such duress.

They "cheated." State and federal governments went all out to get the teachers, eventually charging them with RICO (Racketeer Influenced and Corrupt Organizations Act) violations. This is the law used by prosecutors to attack organized crime. Most of the indicted educators cut deals to lower their legal penalties, and the teachers' unions refused to stand by the members who wouldn't say uncle. The lesson public school teachers are likely to take from this McCarthy era "show trial," is that they had better get with the program. Teach always to the test, and take your medicine if your school is closed. Let the rich and powerful have their way, and let your students sink or swim in the new dispensation.[19]

Schools are also themselves sources of capital accumulation, whether it be by textbook companies, testing material suppliers, or soft drink purveyors. The charter school movement has little to do with improving education and everything to do with using public money to subsidize private interests. Furthermore, and this is true for other consequences of inequality, the political power the wealthy now have allows them to pressure governments at all levels to continually lower their tax burden. This starves governments of revenue and paves the way for conservative arguments in favor of cutbacks in social welfare spending. Close public schools, especially in poor communities, furlough teachers, and demonize the teachers' unions. The rich don't care about this; they send their kids to private schools.

Housing

The impacts of inequality on housing range from obvious to subtle. Public housing has been a dead letter for many years, and rising inequality will keep it on life support into the indefinite future. Governments will be unlikely to fund building rehabilitations or provide money for repairs to the millions of units of substandard and unhealthy apartments and single-family homes. "The Center on Budget and Policy Priorities reports: 'From 2010 to 2012, funding for housing assistance fell by $2.5 billion, or 5.9 percent just in "nominal terms"—i.e., not counting the additional losses due to the effects of inflation—while funds for community development programs fell by $1.5 billion, or 24 percent.

Policymakers cut funds for public housing and housing and community development block grant programs most sharply.'"[20]

Whenever new housing is built, it is more and more for the well-to-do. City governments sometimes give tax breaks to developers for agreeing to include lower-income housing in development projects, but these are honored more in the breach.[21] Rapidly rising wealth at the top means that more space will be devoted to their housing, not just in terms of land use but also in terms of the size of apartments. Little space is used for smaller and cheaper apartments. Economist Moshe Adler writes, "My own calculations show that if Manhattan apartments were limited in size to 1,200 square feet, then, without constructing even one new building, the supply of apartments for ownership would increase by 35 percent and the supply of apartments for rent would increase by 20 percent."[22]

The collapse of the housing market triggered the "Great Recession" that began in the United States in late 2007. However, the freefall in housing prices was itself closely tied to inequality. For at least the past two decades the United States has been prone to speculative bubbles, that is, periods when certain prices rise beyond any rational calculation of how high these prices should be. The last bubble occurred in the housing market, commencing near the beginning of the twenty-first century. Households with modest incomes had seen wages stagnating for many years. To make ends meet, they began to incur debts. Given that the only valuable asset most of these households owned was their home, they began to use it as collateral for loans. At the same time, the Federal Reserve forced interest rates down and Chairman Alan Greenspan sought to engineer a recovery from the recent bursting of the dot.com bubble. Low interest rates and aggressive marketing by banks, spurred on by government propaganda urging home buying, brought forth a rapid escalation of housing demand and construction. Within a couple of years, housing prices began to steadily and then briskly rise. This further encouraged borrowing against the equity homeowners had accumulated. Banks, in turn, ratcheted up lending, lowering their standards for mortgage approval. In addition, lending institutions soon began to invent new financial instruments, presumably to spread the risk of default among many entities, but really to make more money. Mortgages were packaged and split into ever-smaller parts, which were then resold, and resold again. Special insurance devices were designed to further lower risk, but the sale of these took on a life of its own, as they were soon used to speculate on whether a particular business or public agency would default. Everything worked as planned as long as housing prices continued to rise. But the debt that income-strapped homeowners were amassing meant that sooner or later, some would not be able to pay their loans back and would default. This, in fact, happened, and soon the entire process went into reverse, defaults following defaults and then threatening the solvency of the banks and other financial institutions on the hook for all of the loans and exotic new credit schemes they had invented. Had inequality not risen so rapidly, it is doubtful that this bubble could have gotten off the ground.[23]

A recent article in the *Guardian* newspaper illustrates not only another outcome of escalating inequality in the United States but also the intimate connection between the haves and the have nots. As income growth has been siphoned off by the rich, those at the bottom have less money upon which to live. Poverty, by the miserly U.S. standard (three times a rock-bottom food budget, giving a yearly pre-tax income of $23,834 for a family of four in 2013) rose steadily between 2006 and 2012, dropping slightly in 2013. In 2013, 45.3 million people lived in poverty, and of these, 43.8 percent were surviving at one-half the poverty level of income. Rates for black and Hispanic persons were considerably higher: 27.2 percent for Blacks and 23.5 percent for Hispanics.[24]

Poverty causes a multitude of problems for those in its grasp, but for the rich, the large and growing number of poor people is an opportunity. The *Guardian* report is about the growing investment opportunities in trailer parks:

> Trailer parks are big and profitable business—particularly after hundreds of thousands of Americans who lost their homes in the financial crisis created a huge demand for affordable housing. According to U.S. Census figures, more than 20 million people, or 6% of the population, live in trailer parks.[25]

Because towns and cities have become loath to allow more trailer parks to be built and because the demand for housing in them is rising, the value of trailer parks has risen. An owner can make money in two ways—through a capital gain by selling a park at an inflated price, or by raising the rent for residents who have no other housing prospects. Those with the requisite cash can buy a trailer park, immediately raise the rents, collect considerable revenues, and then sell to the next greedy buyer. The following quote from the article speaks clearly to the fact that the wealth at the top relies on the misery at the bottom:

> The number one rule is stated twice, once in the classroom and once on the bus: "Don't make fun of the residents." Welcome to Mobile Home University, a three-day, $2,000 "boot camp" that teaches people from across the U.S. how to make a fortune by buying up trailer parks . . .

It is a market that has not been lost on some of the country's richest and most high-profile investors. Sam Zell's Equity LifeStyle Properties (ELS) is the largest mobile home park owner in America, with controlling interests in nearly 140,000 parks. In 2014, ELS made $777 million in revenue, helping boost Zell's near-$5 billion fortune.

> Warren Buffett, the nation's second-richest man with a $72bn fortune, owns the biggest mobile home manufacturer in the U.S., Clayton Homes, and the two biggest mobile home lenders, 21st Mortgage Corporation and Vanderbilt Mortgage and Finance Company. Buffett's trailer park investments will feature heavily at his annual meeting this weekend, which will be attended by more than 40,000 shareholders in Omaha.[26]

Environment

Inequality affects the environment in multiple ways. The rich buy millions of acres of land, denying others access to it. If their property abuts public domains, it will sometimes be difficult for those with lesser means to use these. Access to beaches is a case in point. "Private Property—Keep Out" signs might be sufficient, even if they are illegal. National parks and monuments are often off-limits to the poor simply because they cannot afford to get to them or to pay admission prices. Private contractors control the lodges and other concessions at the parks, and the greater the share of wealth and income taken by the 1 percent, the more concessionaires will press for closing cheaper accommodations in favor of luxury hotels.[27] These developments parallel exactly the building of the billionaire's park in Manhattan.

Tourism is the lifeblood of many towns. Again, with money flowing constantly to the top, local governments encourage and approve the building of upscale hotels and motels, as well as leisure activities that only those with much disposable income can afford. These are often harmful to the environment. In Moab, Utah, a zip line now passes over the slick red rocks of a local park and jeep and ATV safaris wreak havoc on these same rocks and remote trails. The jeeps and ATVs are ever more powerful and expensive, and the damage they do increases accordingly. Even bicycles harm sensitive landscapes, and as with jeeps, waste energy in transit to these sites. Polluting plane and truck fuel must be accounted for as environmental costs of such sports.[28] Extreme sports of all kinds have proliferated along with inequality, and all of these destroy the environment and waste public safety resources.

The political power of the wealthy has infiltrated every level of government, making politicians increasingly amenable to all sorts of corporate enterprise that destroys nature, from mining to fracking to industrial production of beef, pork, and chicken. It is not unusual for these activities to take place near or even on public lands. Our national forests declare themselves to be "lands of many uses." It is hardly surprising that not a few of these uses serve the interests of those with the most money and political influence.

Monopoly

When a few large firms dominate an industry, we say that they have monopoly power. That is, they have great control over their prices, because they do not face price competition. Prices of the largest businesses move in tandem, almost always rising. When the number of multi-billionaires grows, these money elites will be able, through their control of vast amounts of wealth and the behavior of the corporations in which much of their wealth is embedded, to engineer mergers and acquisitions that enhance their monopoly power. This power, in turn, gives the rich still more political power, which surely will increase inequality further. Monopoly pricing also makes it more profitable to sell fewer units at a higher price than would prevail if there were more suppliers. Everything from music concerts to medical services will then tend to go disproportionately to those with the greatest means to pay.[29]

Let me end this first chapter with two points. First, while this book centers on the facts of inequality and on its harmful social consequences, we cannot overlook the forces that underlie the explosion in this phenomenon itself. As we will see, the essence of the capitalist system drives inequality. The default position of such a system is an unregulated drive to accumulate capital, and this accumulation cannot transpire without the exploitation of workers. If the working class is able to exert sufficient power, this exploitation can be mitigated. However, it, and the resulting inequality, cannot be eliminated unless capital's control is eliminated altogether. Capital's lust for money is insatiable, relentless, ever-vigilant, which is why reforms and victories by the adversaries of the big wealth-holders are always being subverted, and often reversed.

Second, we can write about the evils of inequality all we want, but unless we offer lasting remedies for them, our analysis must remain partial and open to valid criticism. In many of the chapters that follow, I provide both specific policies and a general framework for ending the scourge of inequality.

Notes

1   David Callahan, "The Billionaires' Park," http://nytimes.com/2014/12/01/opinion/the-billionaires-park.html?emc=edit_th_20141201&nl=todaysheadlines&nlid=23341224&_r=0
2   Ibid.
3   http://newrepublic.com/article/120909/barry-dillers-pier-55-park-how-money-changing-city-park

4   See http://forbes.com/billionaires/list/#version:static_search:barry%20diller; http://celeb
     financialwealth.com/diane-von-furstenberg-wealth-annual-income-monthly-income-
     weekly-income-and-daily-income/
5   See Gary S. Becker, Human Capital: A Theoretical and Empirical Analysis, with Special
     Reference to Education, 3rd Edition (Chicago: University of Chicago Press, 1994).
6   Thomas Piketty, Capital in the Twenty-First Century (Cambridge, MA: Belknap Press,
     2014).
7   Alexander Stille, "Grounded by an Income Gap," New York Times, December 15, 2001;
     Michael D. Yates, "The Rich, the Poor, and the Economists," http://monthlyreview.org/
     commentary/the-rich-the-poor-and-the-economists/
8   For an overall critique of neoclassical economics, see Michael D. Yates, Naming the
     System: Inequality and Work in the Global Economy (New York: Monthly Review
     Press, 2002), chapter 5 ("The Neoclassical/Neoliberal Dogma"); Michael D. Yates, "The
     Emperor Has No Clothes But Still He Rules," Monthly Review, 63/2 (June 2011).
9   See Lawrence Mishel, et al., The State of Working America, 12th Edition (Ithaca,
     N.Y.: ILR Press, 2012).
10   http://gawker.com/study-the-u-s-is-an-oligarchy-1563363760
11   Matea Gold, "Koch-backed network aims to spend nearly $1 billion in run-up to 2016,"
     http://washingtonpost.com/politics/koch-backed-network-aims-to-spend-nearly-1-
     billion-on-2016-elections/2015/01/26/77a44654-a513-11e4-a06b-9df2002b86a0_
     story.html
12   To learn in great detail who runs the nation politically, see G. William Domhoff, Who
     Rules America? 7th Edition (New York: McGraw-Hill, 2013) and the useful website
     http://2.ucsc.edu/whorulesamerica/. Also, see Laurence H. Shoup, Wall Street's Think
     Tank: The Council on Foreign Relations and the Empire of Neoliberal Geopolitics,
     1976–2014 (New York: Monthly Review Press, 2015).
13   http://gallup.com/poll/143696/health-disparities-across-incomes-wide-ranging.aspx;
     http://ncbi.nlm.nih.gov/books/NBK62362/
14   http://huppi.com/kangaroo/Inequality&Health.html; http://inequality.org/inequality-
     health/; R. G. Wilkinson and K. E. Pickett, "Income Inequality and Social Dysfunction,"
     Annual Review of Sociology, 35 (2009), 493–511.
15   Nico Pitney, "Scientists find alarming deterioration in DNA of the urban poor," http://
     huffingtonpost.com/2015/05/08/poverty-race-ethnicity-dna-telomeres_n_7228530.
     html
16   See http://org.salsalabs.com/o/307/images/JGIM%20Underinsurance%20Proofs%20
     Un-Corrected%281%29.pdf. Many useful articles can be found on the website of
     Physicians for a National Health Program: http://pnhp.org/. For an excellent analysis
     of the class bias of Obamacare, see Charles Andrews, "The Doctor Will See You Now.
     First, Your Copay: The Erosion of Health Security Under the Affordable Care Act,"
     http://mrzine.monthlyreview.org/2015/andrews290415.html
17   Peter McClaren and Ramin Farahmandpur, "The Pedagogy of Oppression: A Brief
     Look at 'No Child Left Behind,'" Monthly Review, 58/3 (July–August 2006).
18   "Notes From the Editors," Monthly Review, 66/13 (June 2015).
19   The best essay I have read on the convicted Atlanta teachers is http://hatueysashes.
     blogspot.com/2015/04/show-trial-ends-with-prison-for.html
20   Paul Le Blanc and Michael D. Yates, A Freedom Budget for All Americans: Recapturing
     the Promise of the Civil Rights Movement in the Struggle for Economic Justice Today
     (New York: Monthly Review Press, 2013), 198.
21   Charles V. Bagli, "In Program to Spur Affordable Housing, $100 Million Penthouse
     Gets 95% Tax Cut," New York Times, February 1, 2015.

22   Moshe Adler, Economics for the Rest of Us: Debunking the Science that Makes Life
     Dismal (New York: The New Press, 2009), 84.

23   For a detailed and accessible discussion of the forces leading up to the Great Recession,
     as well as the consequences of it, see Fred Magdoff and Michael D. Yates, The ABCs
     of the Economic Crisis: What Working People Need to Know (New York: Monthly
     Review Press, 2009). Also, for good data on the impact of the housing meltdown, see
     Lawrence Mishel, et al., The State of Working America, 12th Edition, 394–398.

24   Carmen DeNavas-Walt and Bernadette D. Proctor, U.S. Census Bureau, Current
     Population Reports, P60–249, Income and Poverty in the United States: 2013
     (Washington, D.C.: U.S. Government Printing Office, 2014).

25   http://theguardian.com/lifeandstyle/2015/may/03/owning-trailer-parks-mobile-home-
     university-investment?CMP=ema_565

26   Ibid.

27   Michael D. Yates, "Wage Slaves in Our National Parks," http://cheapmotelsandahot
     plate.org/2012/06/01/wage-slaves-in-our-national-parks/

28   See Jim Stiles, "Recreation Calls the Shots in Moab," https://hcn.org/wotr/recreation-
     calls-the-shots-in-moab

29   The connections between monopoly power and inequality are developed in Moshe Adler,
     Economics for the Rest of Us.

2
THE GREAT INEQUALITY

If there is one truth that readers should take from this book, it is that there is nothing inevitable or good about inequality. We have it because of the kind of society in which we live. The first step in ending inequality is to grasp its magnitude. Most people have a limited understanding of how wide is the gap between those at the top of the income and wealth ladder and those at the bottom. Americans tell researchers that they would like to see a more equal distribution of wealth, but what they think is the current distribution is woefully incorrect.

The average American believes that the richest fifth own 59 percent of the wealth and that the bottom 40 percent own 9 percent. The reality is strikingly different. The top 20 percent of U.S. households own more than 84 percent of the wealth, and the bottom 40 percent combine for a paltry 0.3 percent. The Walton family, for example, has more wealth than 42 percent of American families combined.

Worse still,

The median American estimated that the CEO-to-worker pay-ratio was 30-to-1, and that ideally, it'd be 7-to-1. The reality? 354-to-1. Fifty years ago, it was 20-to-1.[1]

The second step is to learn what causes inequality and the third is to explore what might be done to change matters. Hopefully, this chapter will help readers begin to take all three steps.

When I told my students that growing inequality of income and wealth would become the dominant political issue of the future, I did not think that the future meant thirty years. Better late than never. The Occupy Wall Street (OWS) uprising put inequality squarely on the political agenda, with the brilliant slogan, "We are the 99 percent." While the "99 percent" includes many well-off persons and not everyone in the top 1 percent is truly rich, the focus on the "1" at the summit of the economic pyramid served to shine a light on those who rule both the economy and the politics of the United States. The 1 percent is a diverse group, but among them, especially at the top, are the men and (a few) women who own controlling interests in our largest businesses, including the financial corporations whose actions precipitated the Great Recession, which officially began in December 2007 and ended in June 2009, and has since morphed into what looks like a long period of slow growth best termed "stagnation." They are also the people whose campaign contributions and prominent positions in Congress, as advisers to the president, and on the Supreme Court, have placed the government firmly on the side of the rich.

Given the prominence that OWS gave to inequality, it is useful to know what causes it.[2] We cannot look just at the facts, dramatic as they might be, and say that something is wrong or that all we need is to take money from the rich and transfer it to the poor. What is needed is a theory of distribution, because this can give us guidance on what political strategy might best confront the underlying forces that generate inequality. Fortunately, economist Eric Schutz, in his timely book *Inequality and Power: The Economics of Class* provides us with such a theory.[3] His argument is simple and straightforward. Those who are rich have advantages that keep them rich, while the poor suffer disadvantages that keep them poor. However, there is a relationship between the two groups, one in which the rich have power over the poor, and this relationship is built into the nature of a capitalist economy and continuously reproduced by it. The supremacy of the dominant group reinforces the existing set of social/property relationships, which serves to further enhance the power of that group relative to all others. It turns out to be no surprise that the rich are the capitalists, and the poor are the workers. Multiple complications must be considered, but these work in general to strengthen the basic power inequality. Therefore, attacking inequality will require nothing less than attacking capitalism itself. There are a host of pragmatic measures that can reduce inequality, but only those that address the system-generated power of the capitalists can strike down the structures that give rise to it in the first place.

Let us preface our interrogation of a theory of inequality with a detailed look at the facts. They are startling. There are many kinds of inequality, but the two most obviously important ones are those of income and wealth. Incomes—normally in a money form but also "in kind," as when part of a worker's pay takes the form of room and board—are flows of cash (or "kind") that go to persons over some period of time, such as a wage per hour or a yearly dividend. Incomes are always unevenly divided in a capitalist economy, and in the United States they are more unequal than in every other rich capitalist country. Since 1980, the year Ronald Reagan became president and helped engineer a savage attack on the working class, income inequality has risen considerably.

Households are physical spaces identified by the Census where people live, excluding institutional spaces like prison cells. Those in a household need not be related. In 2013, according to U.S. Census data, the richest 20 percent of all households received 51 percent of total household money income. The poorest 20 percent got 3.2 percent. A mere three decades ago, in 1980, at the outset of the so-called Reagan Revolution, these shares were 44.1 and 4.2 percent, respectively. Those in the least-affluent households thus lost 23.8 percent of their income share, while the most affluent saw theirs rise by 15.6 percent. The next two poorest quintiles also lost in their shares of the economic pie, while the next richest quintile gained, but not by nearly as much as the top quintile. The Census breaks out the richest 5 percent of households from the top quintile. The income share of the richest 5 percent rose from 16.5 percent in 1980 to 22.2 percent in 2013, a gain of 34.5 percent. In 2013, the share of the top 5 percent was greater than that of the bottom 50 percent of households.[4]

Economists often use a single statistic, the Gini Coefficient, to summarize increases or decreases in inequality or to compare inequality among countries.[5] The Gini is a measure of how far away the actual distribution of income is from one of perfect equality, which would be a distribution in which each income quintile received exactly 20 percent of the total household income pie. In this case, the Gini turns out to equal zero. If, on the other hand, one household got all the income, the distribution would be perfectly unequal, and the Gini equals one. The greater the inequality, the closer is the Gini to one; the more equal, the closer it is to zero. The Gini Coefficient in the United States has been rising for nearly four decades. In 2013, the U.S. Gini was, according to Census calculations, equal to .476. In 1980, it was .403.[6] Most wealthy capitalist nations have coefficients considerably lower than that of the United States. An article on *The Atlantic* website puts U.S. inequality starkly: "Income inequality is more severe in the United States than it is in nearly all of West Africa, North Africa, Europe, and Asia. We're on par with some of the world's most troubled countries, and not far from the perpetual conflict zones of Latin America and Sub-Saharan Africa."[7] Recently, economic historians Walter Schiedel and Steven Friesen estimated that the Gini Coefficient in the Roman Empire at its peak population around 150 C.E. was slightly lower than that of the contemporary United States.[8]

The Census data are based upon sample surveys of households, and these use a definition of income that does not include capital gains (an example would be the sale of a share of stock at a higher price than that at which it was purchased), which go overwhelmingly to high-income households. Therefore, the share of the top quintile is lower than it would be if capital gains income were included. In addition, the Census Bureau has found that non-wage incomes, such as rent, dividends, interest, and profits of unincorporated businesses, are underreported in the surveys, and this again lowers the apparent share of the most well-off households.

Economists Thomas Piketty and Emanuel Saez have used federal income tax data, with their broader definition of income and truer reporting, to provide a more detailed and refined picture of the U.S.

income distribution. Their findings show that the income share, including capital gains, of the richest 1 percent of individuals (note that individual and household incomes are not necessarily the same) was now at its highest level since just before the Great Depression, standing at 23.5 percent in 2007 when the Great Recession began. This share fell during the Great Recession, to 18.1 percent, but it recovered to 20.1 percent in 2013. What is more, it has been rising sharply since 1980, when it was 10 percent. If we take the total gain in household income between 1979 and 2007, 60 percent of it went to the richest 1 percent of individuals, while just 8.6 percent accrued to the poorest 90 percent. An incredible 36 percent found its way into the pockets of the richest 0.1 percent (one-one thousandth of all individuals). Saez found that during the first three years of the recovery (2009–2012) following the Great Recession, the richest 1 percent of income recipients captured 91 percent of total income gains.[9]

Amazingly, there is stark income inequality even at the top of the income distribution. In the United States in 2007, it is estimated that the five best-paid hedge-fund managers "earned" more than all of the CEOs of the Fortune 500 corporations combined. The income of just the top three hedge-fund managers (James Simons, John Paulson, and George Soros) taken together was $9 billion dollars in 2007.[10] In 2013, the top three (Soros, David Tepper, and Steve Cohen) took in $9.8 billion.[9] In early 2015, the U.S. Internal Revenue Service issued a report on income shares for 2012, and investigative reporter and teacher David Cay Johnston has written an eye-opening summary.[11] For the first time, the IRS showed the income share of the richest .1 percent of the top 1 percent. This is .001 times .01 or .00001—the richest one-thousandth percent (.001 percent). What Johnston finds is that the income gap within the richest 1 percent, between those at its bottom and those at its top is widening more than the distance between the 1 percent and 99 percent of Occupy Wall Street fame. These households, which numbered 1,361 in 2012, had an average (mean) income of $161 million. The lowest average annual income in the highest 1 percent, that is, those at the 99th percentile was $434,600. So, the range of incomes in the 1 percent is enormous, with the real money concentrated

at the top. Johnston goes on to say that income growth at the pinnacle
of the 1 percent dwarfs that for the entire rest of this group. Remarkably,
for all of those households between the 90th and the 99.9th percentile,
average income grew by $424,000 (adjusted for inflation), between 2003
and 2012, but that for the richest .001 percent, it rose by $84.6 million.
The author provides a telling way to grasp this:

> Here's a simple way to put that in perspective: Think of the top
> percent having an income ladder with a thousand steps. On the
> lowest rung stand those making $434,600 in 2012. On the 1,000th
> rung are 1,361 very lucky families. For each household on the first
> 999 steps that gained one dollar those on the very top step got
> $200.
>
> The top one-in-a-thousand households captured an astonishing
> 21 percent of the group's income gains. Ponder that for a moment:
> One in a thousand households in the top 1 percent got more than
> a fifth of all the increased income.[12]

To add insult to injury, these fabulously rich households paid a mere
17.6 percent of their income in federal taxes.[13]

Perhaps a story and some striking facts will illustrate just how
fabulously wealthy are today's billionaires and how far removed they
are from everyone else. If a person spent $10,000 a day (my encyclo-
pedia used $1,000 a day, but that was a long time ago), it would take
100,000 days to spend a billion dollars, just under 274 years. In 2009,
Pittsburgh hedge-fund manager, David Tepper, made four billion
dollars.[14] This income, spent at a rate of $10,000 a day and exclusive of
any interest, would last him and his heirs 1,096 years! If we were to
suppose that Mr. Tepper worked 2,000 hours in 2009 (fifty weeks at
forty hours per week), he took in $2,000,000 per hour and $30,000 a
minute. This means that he would have paid his social security tax for
the entire year in about four minutes of his first workday. Today there
are many individuals who, while not as rich as Tepper, make millions
of dollars in a single year, enough money to secure them against any
calamity.

Others are not so fortunate. According to the Census Bureau, "In 2013, 19.9 million people lived in families with an income below one-half of their poverty threshold. They represented 6.3 percent of all people and 43.8 percent of those in poverty."[15] The official poverty level of income in 2013 was $23,550, half of which was $11,775. If we imagine a worker laboring full-time, year-round (2,000 hours of work per year), this would be the equivalent of an hourly wage of $5.88. At this rate, it would take someone nearly three years to earn what Tepper got each minute. Presently, about one-quarter of all jobs in the United States pay an hourly wage rate that would not support a family of four at the official poverty level of income.[16]

If incomes are unequal and becoming more so, the same can be said for a more important, though related, statistic—wealth. Simply put, wealth, for our purposes, is the money value of what we own at a given point in time. It includes houses, cars, computers, cash, stocks, bonds—anything convertible into cash. If we subtract what we owe from what we own, we get net worth. Wealth is important for many reasons. Some types of wealth, such as stocks and bonds, generate income, such as dividends, interest, and capital gains. A good deal of the income of people like David Tepper is saved and converted into wealth, which in turn, generates income, and so on, indefinitely. If incomes are unevenly divided, and if rich households save a bigger fraction of their income than do poor ones, wealth will get steadily more unevenly divided, even if the income distribution remains stable. Wealthy individuals with a lot less than Tepper can live, and live well, without ever working, simply by spending income that derives from their wealth. Some wealth represents possession of the means of production, such as factories, land, banks, and the like, and such ownership is obviously important in terms of economic power. Even more mundane forms of wealth such as automobiles and houses can provide security and aid us in earning our incomes. Wealth can be used as collateral for loans; the more of it we have, the more we can borrow and the more favorable the terms of the loans. Wealth can be inherited and thus passed down, with its advantages intact, to future generations. Our capacities to work and earn wages, on the other hand, die with us.

Sylvia Allegretto of the Economic Policy Institute has done an extended analysis of the current U.S. wealth distribution.[17] In her article, she provides charts and tables that show that in 2009, the top 1 percent of households owned 35.6 percent of net wealth (net worth) and a whopping 42.4 percent of net financial assets (all financial instruments such as stocks, bonds, bank accounts, and all the exotic instruments that helped trigger the Great Recession, minus non-mortgage debt). The bottom 90 percent owned 25 percent of net wealth and 17.3 percent of net financial wealth.[18] The richest 1 percent had 33.1 percent of net worth in 1983 (the chart does not show the numbers for 1980), an increase of 7.5 percent; if we extend our view to the wealthiest 5 percent, we see a rise in share from 58.1 to 63.5 percent, an increase of 9.3 percent. The bottom four-fifths of households suffered a decline in their share of net worth, from 18.7 to 12.8 percent, a loss of nearly 32 percent. Allegretto shows the share of the poorest 20 percent of households; it is negative and declining, meaning that, on average, these households owe more than they own, and the gap between what they own and owe is getting larger. To put these numbers in proper perspective, she notes that the wealth of the "1 percent" is now 225 times larger than the median wealth of all households, the highest ratio on record. It was 131 times larger in 1983.

Allegretto's charts and tables provide three particularly striking facts about wealth. First, as with income at the very top, there is inequality too. For the super wealthy in the "Forbes 400," a list compiled by *Forbes* magazine of the richest persons in the United States, average net worth was $3.2 billion in 2009. However, the top wealth holder of the "400" had wealth fourteen times greater than the average for all 400. In 1982, this ratio was 8.6. Second, the share of households with zero or negative net worth increased by 60 percent between 1983 and 2009; we now have about a quarter of all households in this wealth-less state.

Third, and a critical element in any discussion of inequality, is the disparity in wealth by race. The fraction of black households with no or negative net worth was nearly 40 percent in 2009, almost double the fraction for white households. The median net worth of black households in 2009 was a paltry $2,200, a mere 2 percent of white net worth, which was $97,900; this ratio was three-and-a-half times higher in 1983. The median net financial wealth of black households was $200, remarkably low but an improvement over 1983 when it was zero. So much for the nonsense promoted by conservatives that race no longer matters.

Not much has changed since Allegretto's study. A 2014 analysis of wealth data by economists Emmanuel Saez and Gabriel Zucman found that the wealth share of the wealthiest 10 percent, 1 percent, and .1 percent of households continues to rise steadily. Of considerable interest is that the increase in the share of the wealthiest 10 percent has been due to the disproportionate increase in the share of the richest 1 percent. And similarly, the growth in the share of the wealthiest 1 percent has been the result of the disproportionate increase in the share of the wealthiest .1 percent. The rich keep getting richer, and the extremely rich keep getting richer still.[19] We are seeing the creation of a super-wealth class. Walled off, figuratively and literally, from the rest of U.S. society. And not just from those at the bottom. A recent Pew Research Center report found that in 2013 the wealth of high income families—who are defined, for a family of four, as having yearly income greater than $132,000—have net worth 6.6 times greater than those with middle incomes—defined, for a four-person family, as having annual income greater than $44,000. This is the largest such wealth gap on record. Imagine how much greater is the distance between the middle and the very top, the 1 percent and .1 percent of income earners.[20]

What causes such enormous disparities in income and wealth? Why have they increased so much? Why do they matter? Following Eric Schutz, let us look at these questions systematically. His approach is to start with the theory of mainstream (neoclassical) economists. These economists ignored inequality for decades, but the extent of it has forced them to consider it now. Remember the words of Martin Feldstein, quoted in the Introduction: "Why there has been increasing inequality in this country is one of the big puzzles in our field and has absorbed a lot of intellectual effort . . . But if you ask me whether we should worry about the fact that some people on Wall Street and basketball players are making a lot of money, I say no." As the fine film, *Inside Job*, makes clear, there are a good many economists who still hold this view.

Neoclassical economics believe that a capitalist economy is best conceived as a set of markets in which buyers and sellers act solely out of self-interest, each trying to maximize his or her well-being, which is assumed to be profits in the case of employers and "utility" or "satisfaction" for employees. Each market actor is assumed to face constraints of one kind or another, and each takes these constraints as a given, making choices within them so as to maximize profits or "utility." Ordinarily, the analysis focuses on the choices and not the constraints, but it is the constraints that matter most.

Imagine a man making a labor market decision. Assume that he has complete knowledge of the wages and benefits associated with every occupation he is considering entering. He also knows what it will cost him in terms of schooling and training to be eligible for employment in each occupation, as well as the income he will have to forego by not working while he is getting the necessary schooling and training. Any particular disamenities of an occupation, such as physical danger, are also costs of entering it. Given these considerations, what will he do? He will assess the costs and benefits of each occupation and choose that for which the difference between the two is the largest. Implicit in this scenario is a wage for each occupation that at least covers the cost of entering it. Competition in the marketplace will, in fact, make the wage just equal to the entry cost. An occupation with a wage higher than the entry cost will attract new applicants; this will put downward pressure on the wage and upward pressure on the costs (as more people demand schooling and training). Eventually, in equilibrium as the economists say, the above average wage–cost difference will disappear.

The implication of this theory is not intuitively plausible. It is that, while some workers earn higher wages than others, higher wages must reflect higher entry costs. A doctor, then, is not really better off than a motel room cleaner; in terms of wages minus costs, they are in exactly the same position. What a happy result! At least as far as labor income is concerned, there can be no inequality.

The neoclassical model always seemed implausible to my students. I used to tell them that this is so because it is. As Schutz dramatically shows us, it is not difficult to demolish this theory. First, proponents of mainstream theory do admit to one reason why there might be inequality—if some persons had greater innate ability than others. If you and I appear to face the same wage and entry cost but I have greater innate ability than you, in practice I will face a lower cost because, for example, I will be able to complete a course of education more rapidly than you. Or I will be able to work less hard and get the same amount of work done as you, giving me a psychic income (a non-income "utility") that you will not get. Either way, I will enjoy a permanent advantage over you, one that competition will not eliminate. However, this notion of unequal ability falls to the ground if we cannot know what innate ability is or how it might be measured, neither of which we do know and in all likelihood cannot know. We should note that when neoclassical economists could not explain the wage differentials between white and black workers, some floated the notion that black employees might have less inborn capacity.

Second, wages are not the only type of income. Profits, rents, and interest all must be accounted for. Rent and interest are returns to the ownership of real property and bonds. They have nothing to do with work or ability. You get the income simply because you own the underlying assets; the more of them you own the more income you receive. The market will do nothing to equalize these amounts, and the legerdemain the neoclassical economists use to argue that unequal wage incomes are really equal cannot be employed here. Economists have come up with a number of reasons why profits can be analyzed in the same way as wages, but these also can be easily skewered. Schutz points out, for example, "Profit may be argued to be an indirect return to labor itself, as most people who receive it do so by virtue of having put aside a portion of their labor income which accumulates into the savings that are then invested in one or more firms."[21] Or, "Business owners (and land owners, lenders and other investors) receive property income for the very specific labor they perform of *managing their resources*, obviously a critically necessary productive activity."[22] These arguments, however, run up against the truths that business investment comes overwhelmingly out of retained earnings, and the income a businessperson receives for managing is a wage. And managers are typically hired, especially by the large firms that dominate the economy. The conclusion we must reach is that profits are just another return to the ownership of property. More of it accrues to those who own the most business property, or the stocks that represent such ownership.

Third, when neoclassical economists ignore or make light of the unequal constraints market actors face, they remove from their theory what is most important in decision-making. Constraints take many forms: cultural backgrounds are different; material circumstances are extremely unequal and these shape and condition cultural differences; there are considerable inequalities in the amount of information available to people; some have the power to withhold or manipulate the information available to those contemplating investments in their "human capital"; some have social connections that can give boosts to their career paths; some face racial and/or gender discrimination; labor markets are segmented by monopoly power, and this limits the number of "good" jobs to those in the primary, more monopolized markets; it takes time to unravel any incorrect market decisions we make, and this time may exceed our lifetimes; people can get trapped where they live because they cannot afford to relocate every time an employer moves or some catastrophe occurs; and, of great importance, we have widely different access to the credit so essential for making any kind of investment, and whatever access we have depends critically on the wealth we have available for collateral when we apply for loans.

The upshot of all this is that we make choices subject to constraints over which most of us have little control. And nearly all of the constraints are intimately tied to the material circumstances in which we find ourselves. Since we know conclusively that these material circumstances are unequal, we also know that the outcomes, in terms of income and wealth, will also be unequal, irrespective of whether markets are competitive or whether people have similar or dissimilar innate aptitudes.

Perhaps something I wrote in my book, *Naming the System*, sums up concretely the uselessness of the theory of individual choice in explaining inequality:

In Pittsburgh, Pennsylvania, where I lived for many years, there is an extraordinarily wealthy family, the Hillmans, with a net worth of several billion dollars. One of their homes, along once fashionable Fifth Avenue, is a gorgeous mansion on a magnificent piece of property. About three miles east of this residence is the Homewood section of the city, whose mean streets have been made famous by the writer, John Edgar Wideman. On North Lang Street there is a row of three connected apartments. One of the end apartments has been abandoned to the elements, to the rodents and the drug users. This is gang territory, and if you are African American, you do not go there wearing the wrong colors. Poverty, deep and grinding, is rampant on this street and in this neighborhood, which has one of the nation's highest infant mortality rates.

Consider two children, one born in the Hillman house and another born in the North Lang Street apartment. In the former, there are two rich and influential parents, and in the latter there is a single mother working nights with three small children. Let us ask some basic questions. Which mother will have the best health care, with regular visits to the doctor, medicine if needed, and a healthy diet? Which child is more likely to have a normal birth weight? Which child is more likely to get adequate nutrition and have good health care in early childhood? If the poor child does not have these things, who will return to this child the brain cells lost as a consequence? Which child is more likely to suffer the ill effects of lead poisoning? Which child is more likely to have an older sibling, just 12 years old, be responsible for him when the mother is working at night? Which will be fed cookies for supper and be entertained by an old television set? If the two children get ill in the middle of the night, which one will be more likely to make it to the emergency room in time? Which child will start school speaking standard English, wearing new clothes, and having someone at home to make sure the homework gets done? Which child will travel, and which will barely make it out of the neighborhood?

As the two children grow up, what sort of people will they meet? Which will be more likely to meet persons who will be useful to them when they are seeking admission to college or looking for a job or trying to find funding for a business venture? Which will be more likely to be hit by a stray bullet fired in a war over drug turf? Which will go to the better school? Which will have access to books, magazines, newspapers, and computers in the home? Which one will wear worn-out clothes? Which one will be embarrassed because his clothes smell? Which one will be more likely to have caring teachers who work in well-equipped and safe schools? Which one will be afraid to tell the teacher that he does not have crayons and colored paper at home? Which child will learn the grammar and syntax of the rich? Which child will join a gang? Abuse drugs? Commit a crime? Be harassed by the police because he is black? When these two children face the labor market, which one will be more productive?

To ask these questions is to answer them. And when we consider that this poor child in the United States is better off than two-thirds of the world's population, we must conclude that most of the world's people live in a state of deprivation so extreme that they must be considered to have almost no opportunities at all. They are almost as condemned as the person on death row in a Texas prison.[23]

If individual choices cannot take us very far in explaining inequality, what can? The constraints that we face are enormously unequal, and this takes us further in our quest to discover the roots of inequality. Yet, what is it that structures the constraints themselves? Why is it that we find ourselves in circumstances from which there does not appear to be a way out, even if we are rational, smart, and skilled in making decisions? Schutz puts the problem clearly:

A simple individual choice approach to economic inequality fails utterly as a theory of distribution because it neglects the opportunity side of individual choice. People can only choose from among whatever alternatives are available to them, hence in principle the opportunity side matters as much as the choice side. We have seen how a consideration in-depth of the most important general patterns or contours of opportunities in society and economy takes one far in the direction of a clearer understanding of economic inequality. Yet reflecting on the patterns of opportunity considered in earlier chapters . . . we find the story is still not complete, for we still do not have a complete answer to the question, what determines these patterns of opportunity, from where do they come, or how do they arise?[24]

The problem with the neoclassical perspective is that it is static; at best it can make comparisons of different circumstance or two different points in time, but it cannot tell us the dynamics of the unequal circumstances or how we go from one point in time to another. You and I are in different circumstances because we made different choices and/or did not face the same constraints. For us to be more equal, we would have to make similar choices under the same constraints. Yet, what if whatever it is that generates the life conditions in which we make our choices guarantees that the constraints can never be the same or even altered permanently?

Schutz's approach here is ingenious, and it takes us directly to a consideration of class not just as a condition—as in, you and I are in different social classes—but as a dynamic relationship in which one class exercises power over another so that society is structured in such a way that there can be no escape from persistent inequalities unless the power (class) relationship is confronted directly and abolished. Although we don't usually think this way, it is true that as we make our individual choices, we also collectively make "social choices." That is, we structure the very society that faces us with constraints when we choose. However, to say this is to suggest that we are not at all equal in terms of how society itself is constructed. At the level of society, power is critically important. Here is how Schutz defines power: "If person A can get person B to do something in A's interest by taking advantage of some situation or set of circumstances to which B, were he or she free to choose with full knowledge from among all possible alternatives, would not give full consent, then A has power over B."[25]

Even with this general definition, it is still possible immediately to say some particular things about power. First, power allows a person unilaterally to change another's constraints, and it can, when exercised long enough, change the habits of subordinates so that the latter act automatically in the interests of their masters. Second, those with personal power will inevitably also have social power, and this will allow them to make the rules that all must obey, and these will benefit the powerful. These rules, in turn, may come to seem normal, which lowers any costs the powerful would have to incur to maintain their power. Third, wherever there is power, there can be no democracy, since if there were, such power would be abolished by majority rule.

To make the definition of power concrete, we must examine it in a capitalist context. The most important kind of power is that which employers exert at the workplace. The advantage capitalists have vis-à-vis their employees is as obvious as it is neglected by mainstream economists. Workers do not have the wealth to withstand periods without employment, and while they might quit a particular job, they cannot quit all jobs. In addition, the ownership of businesses gives capitalists the legal right to structure their workplaces (through detailed division of labor, mechanization, close monitoring to ensure maximum intensity, and so forth) so that the amount of labor used is always a good deal less than the supply of workers. This pool of surplus labor, Marx's "reserve army," serves to keep the employed in line, from making excessive wage and hour demands on the bosses. Employers also create artificial job hierarchies to split workers and keep them from seeing their common interests. In larger firms, seemingly impersonal bureaucracies make rules that come to be accepted as inevitable and even fair. All of these things allow employers to extract a surplus of work from their hired hands, a surplus that the employers get to keep. Power always involves a "taking" by the powerful from those without it. What is taken are the fruits of the exercise of their labor time. The control of the labor power of others over a definite period of time, in other words, is the principal basis of economic profit and power under capitalism.

Of course, a "pure" model of power in capitalism, one in which the capitalists merely exploit workers and the analysis stops there, is too simple, even if it remains the essential starting point. There are other social classes to consider, such as managers and professionals. There is a hierarchy of businesses (with the largest monopoly capitals at the top). There is political power, and the power represented by complex social networks and cultural institutions such as colleges and universities and media. Each of these other power hierarchies has a certain degree of independence from the basic economic hierarchy, but each is, in the end, connected to it. Together, they serve inevitably to reinforce it; they make it more impregnable to change by, in large part, making it appear normal, the consequence of human nature, and creative of the best world possible. All of these other power structures make our economic system extraordinarily complex and difficult to penetrate, but they do not negate the essential importance of the capital–labor power inequality. They come into being because of it, and they make it stronger. We cannot understand any of them if we do not grasp it.

Once we have a grasp of the sources of power, and hence inequality, we can ask why both have risen so dramatically in the United States. One mainstream hypothesis assumes that these increases must be due to the skill requirements of certain jobs. Specifically, they argue that the information technology revolution has raised the skill requirements (education and training costs) at the upper end of the wage hierarchy, while these costs at the lower end have either not risen or fallen. Since, according to neoclassical theory, wages equal the costs of entry into an occupation, this implies that wages at the top are rising disproportionately to those at the bottom. However, as Schutz points out, wage inequality began to rise at least a decade before the IT revolution took off. Also, education and training have become more equally distributed, and this should have been reflected in more equality. And if we consider a particular skill group, say those with college degrees in a certain field, inequality has risen within such groups. In addition, as Harry Braverman pointed out many years ago, the de-skilling practices associated with Frederick Taylor are deeply ingrained in what all managements do, so that any argument concerning widespread and long-lasting increases in skill requirements is implausible.[26]

The key to understanding inequality, both between labor and capital and within the wage-earning class, is power. Incomes (and the wealth that can be purchased with incomes) have become so unequal because the power of those at the top has risen at the expense of those at the bottom. Specifically, several things have enhanced the power of those who own and manage capitalist enterprises. IT, for example, has been a boon to the power of top managers, professionals, and the owners themselves. The first two groups have used their superior knowledge of it to extort money from corporate owners, as did those at AIG and other companies who invented and sold billions of dollars of toxic Credit Default Swaps. IT also has enhanced the power of employers to control the labor process, by allowing managers to force greater work intensity. Devices pioneered by Toyota, such as just-in-time inventory, kaizan (constant improvement), and team production have allowed cars to be produced at a rate of one every forty-five seconds. In the modern, IT-driven workplace, there is nowhere to hide. IT continues to churn the labor market, making workers ever more insecure. The constancy of its development and introduction creates a large and growing pool of more or less permanently unemployed persons—perhaps one reason why long-term unemployment remained so high years after the official end of the Great Recession.

Globalization, both alone and in combination with technology, driven by the growing political power of capital, has also significantly increased employer power. Beginning in the mid-1970s, capital intensified its war against labor as it tried to restore falling profits. Its victories in this war allowed it to secure enough political power to alter the global economic landscape through new trade agreements and the elimination of restrictions on international movements of money and investment.

The global economy is now more open for capital, while labor remains much less mobile. This has given employers many more options for production, such as capital export, offshoring, and outsourcing. The exploitation of labor has increased, especially in the Global South where workers can often be paid below the value of their labor power.[27]

Growing inequality has strengthened the tendency toward the monopolization of production in mature capitalist economies. Incomes do not only flow from poorer to richer households; they also move from lesser to greater businesses. Large firms, a small number of which dominate many markets, are best situated to expand globally, and as they do, they become more powerful economically and politically. This power permits them to increase the rate of exploitation of labor, again especially in the Global South, as they can both utilize modern labor process control techniques better than their smaller rivals and exert political pressure more effectively. Their growing and almost total control of mass media creates a modern propaganda system that shapes the culture in a thoroughly pro-capitalist manner, forging a climate in which it is difficult for people to escape being bombarded with the idea that there is no alternative to the terrible things that have been happening to them. Governments are increasingly seen as incapable of doing anything except getting out of the way of the capitalist juggernaut.

The increased political power of capital has harmed labor directly as well. We have seen a weakening of all public programs that make working men and women more secure, from unemployment compensation and public assistance to social security, Medicare, and Medicaid. Labor laws are evermore inadequately enforced, and proposals for better laws never see the light of day. Business-friendly courts gut the common sense meaning of laws that might benefit the majority of people. Antitrust laws have become a dead letter, which steadily eliminates any roadblocks to growing monopoly power, thereby making stronger the inequality-producing trends that weaken the power of workers.

One final factor responsible for the mounting power, income, and wealth of the U.S. ruling class is the growing financialization of the economy. This feature of contemporary capitalism allows for easier attacks on any government that does things that favor workers and the poor. Currency speculation and capital flight are two examples. Furthermore, cash-strapped workers have had to turn to the financial markets to make ends meet, and the new instruments that have been an outgrowth of rampant financialization have allowed the banks to take ample advantage of this, in effect, making profits by taking money directly out of the pockets of the working class.[28]

It is appropriate at this point to ask why inequality matters. There are several compelling reasons. First, from the fact that the power that generates inequality is inherently undemocratic, it follows that societies that exhibit consistently high degrees of inequality, as is true of all capitalist societies, cannot be democratic. As inequality rises in the United States, even the formal democracy we do have becomes less meaningful. Is it not by now, for example, pointless to vote in national elections? Both parties are thoroughly dominated by the hyper-wealthy.

Second, inequality is also harmful to the formation of the social bonds so necessary for human well-being. It isolates us from one another; in effect, there are two worlds, that of the rich and that of the rest of us. The rich exert power over us and, by doing so, deny us our full humanity. As Schutz says: "The concept of alienation clarifies both the extent and the significance of what is lost for those subordinated in social power structures. Not only is their full self-initiative denied . . . but the full development of their faculties and intentions in all other realms of life is thereby stifled and more or less permanently stunted. People . . . manifest behaviors ranging from withdrawal to social or intellectual incompetence, from distraction to aimlessness or apathy, from anger, confusion, depression and anxiety to obsession and neuroses and, in some, violence of one kind or another."[29]

Third, inequality is not good for the economy. As the working class loses ground, its members cannot spend as much money, and this can cause a reduction in the demand for many goods and services, which can dampen capital spending and employment growth. Growing inequality has reduced economic mobility, and this can lower the willingness of workers to put forth as much effort as previously. Fourth, inequality does great damage to the environment. There is no way out of our environmental crisis without a radical change in public policies. Yet, the more inequality there is, which is to say, the greater the power of the well-to-do over everyone else, the less likely is this to happen. Governments become more subservient to business and its growth mania, and they are less likely to combat the rampant consumerism that is the lifeblood of corporations; the more conspicuous and energy-wasting consumption there is; and the more the rich will seek individual ways to insulate themselves from environmental catastrophes.

Modern research suggests a fifth cost of inequality. A growing gap between the top and bottom of the income and wealth distributions causes, in and of itself, a host of problems similar to those we are almost certain are caused by rising unemployment. One researcher studied the states in the United States and found that,

> States with greater inequality in the distribution of income also had higher rates of unemployment, higher rates of incarceration, a higher percentage of people receiving income assistance and food stamps, and a greater percentage of people without medical insurance. Again, the gap between rich and poor was the best predictor, not the average income in the state.
>
> Interestingly, states with greater inequality of income distribution also spent less per person on education, had fewer books per person in the schools, and had poorer educational performance, including worse reading skills, worse math skills, and lower rates of completion of high school.
>
> States with greater inequality of income also had a greater proportion of babies born with low birth weight; higher rates of homicide; higher rates of violent crime; a greater proportion of the population unable to work because of disabilities; a higher proportion of the population using tobacco; and a higher proportion of the population being sedentary (inactive).
>
> Lastly, states with greater inequality of income had higher costs per-person for medical care, and higher costs per person for police protection.[30]

The most difficult part of writing about inequality is explaining to readers what might be done to change things. Here let me paraphrase what Schutz tells us. I will have more to say about this in the last chapter of this book. He delineates three types of solutions:

Traditional measures: more progressive income taxes; greater reliance on estate and gift taxes; higher and inflation-indexed minimum wages; expanded social security, workers' compensation, and unemployment compensation; more aid to needy persons and families; strengthening of Medicare and Medicaid; antitrust enforcement; affirmative action to reduce discrimination; and greater regulation of the media to ensure a broader spectrum of viewpoints.

New thinking: ceilings on executive compensation; encouragement of labor unions (through enforcement of existing laws and amendments to these laws to make organizing workers less burdensome); a universal pension system; universal health care; publicly subsidized "individual development accounts" so that poorer people could buy homes, go to college, or start a business; compensatory spending on local public education and more federal aid for higher education; abolition of corporate personhood; a pluralistic media system; proportional political representation; and a full-employment jobs policy or a basic income entitlement to help break the jobs–income nexus.

More radical changes: socialized investment aimed at the public interest as determined by some sort of democratic decision-making process; a close look at socialist economies to see what they did and have done right (Schutz points out that after recovery from the Second World War, there was no unemployment, homelessness, or illiteracy in the Soviet Union); and consideration of moving toward some form of socialism, such as market socialism or democratic worker-managed firms. The Yugoslav experience offers a good deal of encouragement to proponents of the second of these, and Venezuela's promotion of local and regional communal government with popular decision-making does as well.

Many of Schutz's suggestions are worthwhile goals which radicals could fight to achieve. Yet there is something unsatisfactory about his discussion. He devotes a good part of his book to an elaboration of the dynamic nature of class domination, of how and why power is exercised by one class over another and, in the process, society is structured in such a way that this domination is replicated from one point in time to the next. It would seem necessary, then, to put this analysis in reverse and ask how the self-sustaining set of mechanisms that nourish this system can be unraveled so that working people can develop the power needed to destroy it. Certainly workers have organized and done any number of things to at least improve their daily lives. What has worked? What has not? Which activities have undermined capitalist class power and which have reinforced it? Perhaps this is too much to ask. The Occupy Wall Street uprising, the Wisconsin events of 2011, and all of the revolts that have taken place from Egypt to China, show us that the power of the 1 percent never goes unchallenged. It is our job to push the struggle forward and not just make suggestions.

Eric Schutz's book and my own hard-won grasp of how capitalist economies work make it clear to me that mainstream economics, in both its extreme free-market and liberal forms, can neither explain inequality nor tell us anything meaningful about eliminating it. For this, we need a radical theory, one that gets to the root of the problem. We have to focus on power rooted in the nature of the capitalist economy.

Notes

1   http://scientificamerican.com/article/economic-inequality-it-s-far-worse-than-you-think/
2   A recent Pew Research Center survey indicates that a growing proportion of people in the United States see a sharp class conflict between rich and poor. See Rich Morin, "Rising Share of Americans See Conflict Between Rich and Poor," Pew Research Center, January 11, 2012, http://pewsocialtrends.org
3   Eric A. Schutz, Inequality and Power: The Economics of Class (London: Routledge, 2011).
4   U.S. Census Bureau, Income and Poverty in the United States: 2013 (Washington D.C.: Government Printing Office, 2014).
5   The Gini Coefficient is named after Italian statistician and sociologist, Corrado Gini, 1884–1965. He was a noted fascist, theoretician, and ideologue, who wrote a book titled The Scientific Basis of Fascism, an oxymoronic title if ever there was one.
6   U.S. Bureau of Census, 2013.
7   See Max Fisher, "Map: U.S. Ranks Near Bottom on Income Inequality," The Atlantic, September 19, 2011, http://theatlantic.com.
8   Walter Scheidel and Steven J. Friesen, "The Size of the Economy and the Distribution of Income in the Roman Empire," Journal of Roman Studies 99 (2009): 61–91.
9   The data in this paragraph are taken from "Share of the Nation's Income Earned by the Top 1 Percent," New York Times, October 25, 2011, http://nytimes.com.; Josh Bivens and Lawrence Mishel, "Occupy Wall Streeters are right about skewed economic rewards in the United States," October 26, 2011, http://epi.org; Emmauel Saez, "Striking it Richer: The Evolution of Top Incomes in the United States (updated with 2012 preliminary estimates), http://eml.berkeley.edu/~saez/saez-UStopincomes-2012.pdf; file:///C:/Users/michael/Downloads/saez-UStopincomes-2013.pdf; and The World Top Income Database, http://topincomes.g-mond.parisschoolofeconomics.eu/

10   See Nelson D. Schwartz and Louise Story, "Pay of Hedge Fund Managers Roared Back Last Year," New York Times, March 31, 2010, http://nytimes.com; http://forbes.com/sites/nathanvardi/2014/02/26/the-highest-earning-hedge-fund-managers-and-traders/. There is a useful article in the New York Times that points out that there is a very wide range of incomes among the top 1 percent. Unlike the richest 0.1 percent, not all in this group can be described as extremely rich or wealthy. Still, none of them will starve any time soon. It is interesting to read how these people see themselves, often remarking on how hard they work and, by implication, how deserving they are of their incomes and lifestyles. See Shaila Dawan and Robert Gebeloff, "Among the Wealthiest One Percent, Many Variations," New York Times, January 14, 2012, http://nytimes.com. Note the confusion in the title between wealth and income. The influential liberal economist Paul Krugman notes on his blog that the richest 0.1 percent are not a diverse group. See "But The Top 0.1 Percent Isn't Diverse," New York Times, January 15, 2012, http://krugman.blogs.nytimes.com.

11   David Cay Johnston, "The top .001 percent are different from you and me," http://america.aljazeera.com/opinions/2015/6/the-top-001-percent-are-different-from-you-and-me.html

12   Ibid.

13   Ibid.

14   Schwartz and Story, 2010.

15   U.S. Census Bureau, 2013.

16   Lawrence Mishel, et al., The State of Working America, 12th Edition (Ithaca, NY, 2012).

17   Sylvia A. Allegretto, "The State of Working America's Wealth, 2011: Through Volatility and Turmoil, the Gap Widens," EPI Briefing Paper #292, March 23, 2011, http://epi.org.

18   Economist Edward N. Wolff gives the following breakdown of U.S. assets, with the share owned by the 1 percent.

Asset Class	Share of Top 1% in 2010
Stocks and Mutual Funds	48.8%
Financial Securities	64.4%
Trusts	38.0%
Business Equity	61.4%
Non-home Real Estate	35.5%

Edward N. Wolff, "The Asset Price Meltdown and the Wealth of the Middle Class," NBER Working Paper Series, Working Paper 18559, 2012, http:/nber.org/papers/w18559.pdf, 57, Table 9. Business equity refers to businesses that are not corporations, such as partnerships and sole proprietorships.

19   Emmanuel Saez and Gabriel Zucman, "Wealth Inequality in the United States since 1913," http://gabriel-zucman.eu/files/SaezZucman2014Slides.pdf

20   http://pewresearch.org/fact-tank/2014/12/17/wealth-gap-upper-middle-income/

21   Schutz, 2011, 85.

22   Ibid., 86 (emphasis in original).

23   Michael D. Yates, Naming the System: Inequality and Work in the Global Economy (New York: Monthly Review Press, 2002), 58–59.

24   Schutz, 2011, 63.

25   Ibid., 66.

26   Harry Braverman, Labor and Monopoly Capital: The Degradation of Labor in the Twentieth Century (New York: Monthly Review Press, 1974).

27 This has been stressed in an important recent Review of the Month. See John Bellamy Foster, Robert W. McChesney, and R. Jamil Jonna, "The Global Reserve Army of Labor and the New Imperialism," *Monthly Review* 63, no. 6 (November 2011), 1–31.

28 See the useful essay by Costas Lapavitsas, "Financialisation and Capitalist Accumulation: Structural Accounts of the Crisis of 2007–9," Research on Money and Finance, Discussion Paper no 16, Department of Economics, School of Oriental and African Studies, University of London, February 2010, http://se.ruc.edu.cn

29 Schutz, 2011, 162.

30 See Peter Montague, "Economic Inequality and Health," http://huppi.com.

3
ALL THE ECONOMICS YOU NEED TO KNOW IN ONE LESSON

The previous chapter gave readers a summary indictment of main-stream economics, with special attention to inequality. Here, through a story, I provide a more general critique. Economists use a language of obscurity, with special concepts that give the discipline an air of scientific objectivity. Once at a seminar in graduate school, a professor opined that all economists were physicists, a statement that would have shocked the latter. Economics lost its claim to objectivity a long time ago. It is no more a science than is astrology. Here is something to think about. If there is something that the working class believes to be true, for example, that a higher minimum wage would be a good thing, you can bet that neoclassical economists will say it is a bad thing. I used to tell my students that it was a safe bet to believe the opposite of what any top politician said. The same can be said for the oft-quoted statements of economists. We tend to think that foolish comments made by economists reflect a conservative, libertarian perspective, as, for example, when some practitioner of the "dismal science argues that there is no role for government provision of essential public services, such as education. However, liberal economists hold to the same basic premises as do their conservative counterparts. Here is something from noted liberal economist and winner of the Nobel award in Economics, Joseph Stiglitz when he addressed Occupy Wall Street protesters:

"You are right to be indignant. The fact is that the system is not working right. It is not right that we have so many people without jobs when we have so many needs that we have to fulfill. It's not right that we are throwing people out of their houses when we have so many homeless people. Our financial markets have an important role to play. They're supposed to allocate capital, manage risks. We are bearing the costs of their misdeeds. There's a system where we've socialized losses and privatized gains. That's not capitalism; that's not a market economy. That's a distorted economy, and if we continue with that, we won't succeed in growing, and we won't succeed in creating a just society."

I criticized Stiglitz's remarks as follows:

> Almost every sentence after the first one is wrong. The sentences about the unemployed and the homeless would be fine on their own, but unfortunately they follow the one that says "the system is not working right." How so? It is working exactly as capitalist systems work. They have always been marked by poles of wealth and poverty, periods of speculative bubbles followed by recessions or depressions, overworked employees and reserve armies of labor, a few winners and many losers, alienating workplaces, the theft of peasant lands, despoiled environments, in a word, the rule of capital. Losses are always socialized, and gains are always privatized. It is impossible to create a society that is both just and capitalist.[1]

This chapter helps explain the last sentence of this quote.

Karen and I were hiking in Santa Fe, New Mexico, on the Atalaya Mountain Trail, which begins in the parking lot of St. John's College. This school, like its sister institution in Annapolis, Maryland, is dedicated to a "Great Books" program. Students read and discuss the "great books" of Western Civilization, beginning with the ancient

Greeks, while at the same time studying languages and sciences. The goal of the college is to provide an education that seeks "to free men and women from the tyrannies of unexamined opinions and inherited prejudices. It also endeavors to enable them to make intelligent, free choices concerning the ends and means of both public and private life."

Economics as taught in our colleges and universities and propounded by our pundits and politicians is a good example of a tyranny of "unexamined opinions and inherited prejudices." Ironically, on our hike we met a man who embodied this tyranny. We had stopped to catch our breath on the steep path. Santa Fe is more than 7,000 feet above sea level, and we had not yet acclimated to the altitude. An older man was hiking with some friends, and when he saw us he said "hello." We struck up a conversation, and he asked me what I was doing in Santa Fe. I told him that I was a writer and journalist and we were traveling around the United States gathering information for a travel book to be written from the perspective of an economist. He asked us what we had been observing in our travels. We told him that the three things that stood out most were environmental degradation, suburban sprawl, and growing economic inequality.

I could tell by his demeanor that he did not agree with what we were saying. When we finished, he said that he had a different take on things. He thought that almost everything was getting better. He said that he had been born in Phoenix, Arizona, in 1934, and the air was better today than then, even though there were two million more people there. People were living longer and were healthier than ever before. What especially impressed him was the remarkable distribution system developed by modern retailers. People could get almost anything they wanted anywhere in the country, quickly and efficiently. "Why," he said, "almost everyone in the country lives within an hour of a Wal-Mart Supercenter." After we said that organic food was expensive and hard to get in much of the country, he launched into a long story about his battle against prostate cancer. He said that he had radically altered his diet and was eating natural foods, including organic vegetable juices purchased cheaply at Wal-Mart Supercenters. He suggested that anyone could do the same.

While we were talking, two more of his companions joined us. One of them said, "I see you have met the professor." My interlocutor also had a Ph.D. in Economics and had also taught in a college for a few years. I thought to myself, "Well, that explains a lot."

The Dismal Science

Economics is a peculiar discipline. The dominant economic theory is called the "neoclassical" theory; it is the only one taught in all but a handful of graduate schools. It is the one I was taught, and it is the one the economist we met in Santa Fe learned. It is preached with a zeal and demand for conformity that has led critics to characterize it as a religious cult. Newly-minted Ph.D.s leave school convinced that they have a special knowledge unavailable to the ordinary person, and they devote themselves to giving this knowledge to others.

The main trick used by professors of economics is to draw their pupils into a make-believe world and then convince them that this is a good approximation to the real one, enough so that the world in which we live can be studied effectively by analyzing the fantasy construct. In fact, the professors also claim that this pretend world is a good approximation not just of where we live today but of that of any time in human existence, so that any society can be studied through its lens. To them the neoclassical theory is as universal and timeless as the theories of Einstein. They see economics as the physics of society.

The economists take their analysis one step further. The hypothetical world of their theory is in all important respects ideal, the best we could have. Therefore any deviation from it that we observe in the realm of existence should, in the interest of human happiness, be eliminated.

It is a curious thing to say that something should change in the living world because it does not conform to a creation that does not, and, as we shall see, could never, exist. For example, a minimum wage set by the government interferes with the efficient operation of the ideal world by causing a loss of employment. The neoclassical economists then conclude that we should not have a minimum wage in the actually existing world. Or, the economists conflate the ideal economy of their theory with the real economy, which is capitalism. Since the imaginary economy is good, so too is capitalism. It is no wonder that economics has been compared to religion. To hold such views requires a strong faith.

It is instructive to look carefully at the model economy of economic theory. What the economists do is make a set of restrictive assumptions. They say, "let us assume we have an economy with the following features." They then list these features and trace out their logical economic consequences.

According to the economists, an economy is defined as a system of markets, that is, as the entire set of actions we call buying and selling. They assume that in every market for goods and services (called product markets) and in every market for labor, land, and capital goods (called factor markets), there are numerous independent and isolated buyers and sellers. They further assume that each of these buyers and sellers is a single-minded "maximizer," fixated in all of his or her actions on getting the most of something. Sellers of goods and services, business firms, are assumed to be trying to maximize their profits. Each business firm is assumed to be the equivalent of an individual; the relationships among people inside the firm are ignored and presumed to have nothing to do with the firm's behavior. Buyers of goods and services are labeled consumers, and are assumed to be trying to maximize their "utility," the satisfaction they get from consuming. If consumers are faced with two collections of goods and services with the same price, they will always pick the one that makes them happier. If the two collections give the same happiness, they will always choose the cheaper one.

In the factor markets, the buyers are business firms (the sellers in product markets), and they try to maximize profits by purchasing labor and the other building blocks of production only when these inputs add more to firm revenue than to firm cost. For workers to be hired, in other words, they must be productive enough to justify their pay. It follows that workers will not be hired if they are not productive enough or if they demand too high a wage rate.

The main sellers in factor markets are workers trying to market their ability to work. They supply their labor only if the wage offered by employers is greater than the joy they get from not working. Like consumers, they try to maximize their utility, by dividing their time between work and free time in such a way so that they are happier than if they had divided it any other way.

The economists assume that many thousands of independent and selfish buyers and sellers meet in thousands of market places and try to strike bargains. Each buyer and seller is assumed to be such an insignificant part of any market that not one of them can have any influence on what happens in that market. If one buyer decides to purchase one more unit, this buyer's actions cannot create a shortage of the product for sale and make its price rise. The same argument holds for all sellers as well.

The end result of the haggling in the marketplaces by all the buyers and sellers is that there is established in each market a "just right" price and a "just right" amount of each good and service produced. This happens because each buyer and seller acts solely in self-interest. If a price is too high, the sellers will lower their prices rather than not sell the product. If the price is too low, buyers will offer higher prices rather than do without something that gives them "utility." In the end, each price is neither too high nor too low, but "just right." The amounts supplied are "just right" for similar reasons. If too much is supplied, the price will fall and less will be supplied by profit-seeking firms. If too little is supplied, the price will rise and more will be supplied.

The markets, then, deliver prices and quantities for all goods and services (and for all factors of production, since the same processes are working there too) that are optimal. No other prices and quantities are "just right." The "just right" prices and quantities are called "equilibrium" prices and quantities, and these are the ones the markets give us.

The great thing about all this, according to the economists, is that it occurs without any human planning. No conscious human action is needed; the markets work automatically. As one of the gurus of the economists, Adam Smith, put it, it is as if there is an "invisible hand" guiding the selfish actions of the buyers and sellers toward an optimal outcome.

So far, the economists have assumed that there are large numbers of buyers and sellers in every market, so many that no individual actor in any market can make anything happen by its own actions. They have also assumed that all buyers and sellers act strictly out of self-interest, always trying to maximize something, whether it be profits or happiness. However, other assumptions are needed for the markets in the economists' model economy to perform optimally. Each participant in the marketplace must be independent of every other participant. For example, what one firm does must not enter into the profit-maximizing calculations of any other firm in a market. If one company wants to lower its price because there is a glut of the product in the market, it might hesitate to do so if it thinks that its rivals will start a price war if it does.

Every player in every market also must have complete knowledge concerning everything that might influence his or her decisions. It is difficult to make rational decisions or assume that choices are free when market actors lack available information, either because they don't know it is available or because someone else is monopolizing it.

How does neoclassical economics explain the large and rising inequality, uninspiring jobs, and environmental degradation we see everywhere in the United States? The analysis of the imaginary economy, which is at the heart of the theory, provides the answers. There are two possibilities. An answer might flow directly from the analysis of the ideal economy. Or the world of reality might not conform to that of the ideal one, and this could be the cause of the problem.

Let's look at inequality. Since in the imaginary world, people are rewarded financially according to their productivity, those with low incomes must be less productive than those with high ones. Or, those who are poor might have stronger desires for leisure than those who earn large incomes. In either case, low wages or poverty are the direct result of choices made by individuals. People might have decided not to do the things that would make them more productive, such as obtain more education and training. Those who choose not to become computer literate cannot expect to land a high-tech job.

It could also be true that society's decision-makers, those in government, for example, have, perhaps out of ignorance or an uninformed desire to "do good," created barriers to the making of better choices. The government might have mandated that employers pay a minimum wage, thus denying employment to anyone not productive enough to justify an employer paying that wage. Or perhaps the government has legislated money transfers to the poor, to help them out of poverty, without realizing that this will encourage them to be lazy and unwilling to work hard when they can get money without effort.

The theory provides two types of solutions to inequality. First, if some of us cannot improve our productivity because we are too poor to buy more education or training, the government can enact laws and programs that make it easier for us to do so. Low interest loans to students would be a good example. Subsidies to employers who hire and train the less advantaged would be another. Second, if there are currently in place public policies that have the effect of harming those who have low wages or are poor (harming them in the ideal world of the theory, that is), then these should be eliminated. Minimum wage laws and welfare programs would be two good examples.

What about bad jobs, those held mainly by those with low incomes? Economists have approached this problem in two ways. It is implied in the theory of the make-believe economy that work is inherently bad. People labor only to get the money necessary to buy the things that give them satisfaction or "utility." Work, itself, gives us only dissatisfaction or "disutility"; this is why we must receive a wage to work. So there is no use in complaining that jobs don't use our full human capacities; it is not possible that they could.

This rather biblical notion of work begs a question: why are some jobs so much worse than others? Here the theory must do some fancy footwork. The basic idea is similar to the premise of the movie, *Field of Dreams.* Build a baseball field in the cornfields of Iowa, and fans will flock to it. If people want better jobs, all they need to do is make themselves available for them. As potential employers see that there are hordes of people ready to do meaningful work, they will note that they can now supply such jobs at wages that will ensure them a good profit. The implication of this analysis is that there are not more good jobs because workers don't want them. Therefore, employers have no incentive to offer them. If it were the case that some workers who want good jobs can't afford to accept the lower wages that would initially be necessary of employers to supply the better jobs, the government could again offer subsidies to employers.

Thousands of articles have been written by economists on the environment. Much of it revolves around the so-called "tragedy of the commons." In the make believe economy of the theory, every bit of property—the land, the air, and the seas—is private property. All of the selfish actors in the markets do everything in their power to preserve their property, and as a result the society as a whole benefits. Whenever there is common property, each person suffers no individual cost if he or she uses it up. You won't litter your yard, but you might toss trash on a public beach or in a park. Only when property is private is there an incentive, for those who own it, to preserve it. Here is one situation in which the real world differs from the ideal world that cries out for an easy solution. The air cannot literally be made into private property, but people can be forced to treat it as if it were. If companies had to pay to pollute the atmosphere, they would either produce a smaller quantity of polluting output (emissions from power plants, for example), or they would find cost-effective ways to reduce pollution. In other words, it is necessary to create market conditions for situations in which previously something could be used without cost. To take another example, consider cars. Auto companies and consumers bear only part of the entire cost of car production and use. Society as a whole bears the cost of auto emissions, acid rain, and so forth. The solution is to privatize the costs society bears, perhaps by taxing gasoline to push up the price and force conservation, or charging high tolls for road use.

It is beyond the scope of this chapter to provide a full-scale critique of mainstream economics. However, if neoclassical economics were a science, its practitioners would subject the theory to rigorous tests and reject it if it proved unable to pass them. Perhaps the reason they do not is that the theory has repeatedly proven itself a poor model of reality, failing test after test. There is no evidence that a higher minimum wage causes a loss of employment, and there is no correlation between a worker's wages and a worker's productivity. Providing people with needed resources, as in a welfare system, does not cause them to use their time unproductively. Evidence does not support the hypothesis that jobs requiring skills are increasing despite the fact that hundreds of millions of people would like them. And there is no evidence that people inevitably destroy property held in common or that making property private guarantees that it will be used in a socially beneficial manner.[2]

Yet the neoclassical theory is taught universally in our colleges and universities, and every economic pundit and economic adviser in government is a believer in the theory. Why is this so? Why could nothing I might have said changed the mind of the economist hiker I met in Santa Fe? I think the reason is that neoclassical economics serves as a gigantic propaganda device aimed at covering up the power of those with money and convincing the rest of us that the bad things happening to us are either inevitable or our own fault. You are rich because you are more productive (and hence deserving) than I. Or you are innately more future-oriented than I; you go to school so you will be productive in the future, while I would rather party now and have a menial job later. If things are going to hell in a handbasket, it is because the real world economy has not been structured to be exactly like that of the ideal economy of the theory. It's my fault, or the government's fault, or it is human nature. The fault never lies with the system itself. This provides the best possible cover for the grotesque wealth of the few, the rotten jobs of the many, and the ruination of the environment.

Toward the Truth

They say that the truth sets us free. Well, here is the truth about the economy. The economy Karen and I have witnessed firsthand for the past fourteen years is a capitalist economy. In such an economy the society's productive wealth is owned by a small fraction of the population. This property is protected by the law, which means that it is secured ultimately by police force, by the state's monopoly on the legal use of violence. The many own no or very little productive property and must depend on the few for their daily bread. This dependence takes the form of offering to the owners their ability to work in exchange for a wage. However, this exchange is not and cannot be one between equals; the party owning what the other party needs has a built-in advantage. Employers use their superior bargaining position to "negotiate" a wage and conditions of employment that guarantee them the ability to extract from workers an amount of labor sufficient not only to pay the workers' wages and replace the capital used up in production but also to generate a surplus above costs. Workers are forced by the fact that they own nothing to work a number of hours greater than those that would pay their wages and the capital costs, and they must give up the output produced during these "surplus" hours to their employer. The employer owns all of the output, simply because the employer owns the business.

The surplus hours workers are compelled to labor are the source of the employers' profits. If the workers had controlled production, they may well have chosen to supply surplus hours (for repairs and to generate funds necessary for the business's expansion), but the decision would have been theirs and not someone else's. In capitalism, the owners own the output, and therefore they own the profits that come from the surplus labor. These profits are extracted from workers whether they like it or not.

Profits are the motor force of capitalist economies. Each business establishment is in a dog-eat-dog competition with other businesses— locally, nationally, and internationally. This competition dictates to the owners of each business that they must use the profits to make the business grow. A company that doesn't get as much profit as possible from the labor of its workers and use this profit to expand will not survive the relentless competition. A company that does not survive will not confer on its owners all the prerequisites of success in capitalism: consumer goods, status, and political power. No wonder owners will do just about anything to ensure the survival and growth of their companies.

To extract profits and grow, corporate owners must try to put downward pressure on wages, to prevent them from increasing at a pace that eats into surplus labor time. They are helped in this by their political power; they can pressure the government, often successfully, to pass laws and utilize its police power to prevent or make it hard for workers to organize to force up their wages and improve their conditions of employment. They are also aided by the strong tendency of capitalist economies to create large reserves of surplus labor, a "reserve army of the unemployed." This reserve is produced by the removal of people from farming (often by force), by the continual mechanization of production, by employer use of labor-saving and de-skilling techniques, by shifting production around the world, and by the tendency of capitalist economies to sink into periodic recessions and depressions. Unemployed labor, including full-time homemakers and prisoners, is available to replace employed workers or at least keep them from demanding too much money, shorter hours, or better working conditions. The education system guarantees that nearly everyone in the reserve army has the capacity to do a variety of jobs.

Because profits are what make capitalist economies tick, and because they come from surplus labor, it behooves employers to exert maximum control over workers. This is done primarily by structuring workplaces in such a way that workers have as little opportunity to interfere with production as possible. What workers do at work—how they perform their jobs, at what pace, and with what intensity—is called the labor process. Employers must control this if they are to make money. Control is the essence of capitalist management.

We need only grasp two concepts to understand modern work. The first is the Babbage Principle and the second is Taylorism. The inventor and manufacturer Charles Babbage showed that an employer intent on making money must organize work so that the amount of skilled labor employed is minimized. If a job requires both skilled and unskilled work, don't allow the skilled worker to do the unskilled parts. Skilled labor is expensive; unskilled is not. A skilled metalsmith executes several steps to make a large batch of tin funnels: making a template, tracing the design on sheets of metal, cutting out the funnel shapes, bending the metal, connecting the ends, and finishing and polishing the funnels. Babbage taught employers to use unskilled laborers to repetitively perform just one of the last five steps, or "details," of the task of funnel-making. Use cheap labor to replace expensive labor wherever possible. The Babbage Principle is a fundamental technique of capitalist management; few jobs are immune to it.

Taylorism is the name given to the management theory developed by Frederick W. Taylor. Taylor, the son of well-to-do Philadelphia Quakers, was sent to work by his father in a machine shop following an emotional collapse. There he was able to capitalize on his obsessive-compulsive personality in a war against the skilled machinists. After he learned the machinists' trade, he was made foreman and began a lifelong campaign to find and enforce the "one best way" to do the work. Taylor became the founder and chief agitator for "scientific management." Despite its high-sounding name, scientific management aims to systematize the Babbage Principle by placing all control over work processes in the hands of the employer. First, management, through the employment of industrial engineers, studies in minute detail what each worker does. Jobs are broken down into their fundamental motions. Then management writes a detailed description of each job's motions, reorganizing them to minimize the time it takes to do each one. The employer next orders every worker to do the work exactly as the engineers say it should be done, using the Babbage Principle whenever possible. By systematic study of work and a willingness to fire recalcitrant workers, Taylor said that management could gain a monopoly of work knowledge and use this to control the entire work process. Taylor taught, and employers were apt pupils. Profits ultimately depend upon the ability of employers to control their workers. Skilled workers are difficult to control, so their proficiencies must be destroyed.

To the capitalist mind, all objects are thought of in terms of their money cost. All things are commodities, to be bought and sold. Whatever else something might be is irrelevant in terms of what is most important to the system, namely the accumulation of capital, the extraction of maximum profits from labor and the use of these profits to achieve maximum growth of capital. We have just seen that our capacity to work is a commodity, bought at the lowest price possible and controlled and exploited to the maximum extent possible. However, there are other inputs that must be purchased besides labor. And these inputs as well as the commodities needed by workers for their survival (food, clothing, shelter) are either an intrinsic part of the natural world or produced in conjunction with it. Coal and iron must be removed from the earth before they can be used to produce steel. Ground must be planted before food can be produced; trees must be cut down or cleared before houses can be built. What is more, all production alters the natural world. The energy produced at a power plant throws all sorts of substances into the atmosphere. Some crops may deplete the soil of its nutrients. The production and use of some products can even alter climates.

All production affects nature, and economic systems prior to capitalism damaged the environment. However, two features of capitalism radically distinguish it from all previous political economies. First, capitalism produces goods and services on a historically unimaginable scale. Even if employers tried their best not to harm nature, their collective size would make the task daunting. But there is a second unique feature of capitalism. Everything is viewed through a calculus of private cost. Or to put it in more academic language, capitalism tends to commodify everything, to turn every object into something for sale. Nothing else matters except that resources be available when needed and at a low price. Lumber companies want trees irrespective of what other functions these trees might serve or that they might possess a beauty worth contemplating. If companies can get away with dumping wastes into our rivers and oceans or into the air, they will, figuring that if they do not some rival might. Dangerous products will be foisted on the public, even if the harm they might do is known by the producing company, as long as the monetary gain from doing so is greater than any cost arising from lawsuits or other consumer actions. The political power that modern giant corporations wield insulates them from severe governmental regulation or legal penalties.

The Proof of the Pudding Is in the Eating

If what I have said about capitalism is true, what would we expect to see with respect to inequality, jobs, and the environment? With a small group of people owning and having near absolute control over society's productive resources, it is inevitable that there will be large income inequalities. Productive property (land, buildings, machinery, factories, and the like) has been unequally distributed from the beginning of capitalism. Because this property generates income (rents, interest, and profits), these will be unevenly divided as well. Unless workers are organized, the very nature of the system confers so much economic and political power on the owners that they are able to leverage their initial economic advantages and augment them. There will be significant impediments to the organization of workers, including the reserve army of labor, so under typical conditions, capitalist economies will exhibit large and often growing inequalities of wealth and income. As we saw in Chapter 1, these will translate into many related inequalities.

What about jobs? Today the Babbage Principle and Taylorism are built into every workplace and are so common that they are taken for granted. Almost no jobs are immune to them; they might be so for a while but not over the long haul. This means that there will be few good jobs available in a capitalist society. Among all the animals, human beings are unique in their ability to transform the world around them by their labor. This ability, in turn, hinges on the human capability to conceptualize what they do before doing it. We can think about our work, plan it out beforehand. This gives us enjoyment as well as lots of output to consume. Unfortunately, capitalism blocks us from taking advantage of our innate human capacities.

There is no reason to expect that capitalism will encourage wise social use of the environment. Quite the contrary, if the natural world is seen merely as a set of exploitable commodities, we would expect to see a short-term profit orientation that views resources, and human beings, as expendable.

The evidence in support of my analysis of capitalism is overwhelming. Just consider the following facts:

1. According to the World Bank, in 2011, just over one billion people lived on $1.25 per day or less. This represents 17 percent of the inhabitants of the world's poor countries. 2.2 billion survived on $2 per day or less.[3] This is about 40 percent of the earth's population. Even supposing that some of these people get some goods and

services outside of the money economy and that prices for some foodstuffs and other necessities are very low, these are appalling numbers.

2. About 9 percent of the world's population gets about one-half of world income. The bottom half collects 7 percent. Globally inequality has been rising, and the world's Gini Coefficient (among individuals) is now an amazing 70. Former World Bank economist and path-breaking analyst of global inequality Branko Milanovic wrote "This is almost certainly the highest level of relative, and certainly absolute, global inequality at any point in human history."[4]

3. The 12 percent of global population living in Western Europe and North America account for 60 percent of total private consumer spending, while the third of the world living in South Asia and sub-Saharan Africa get just 3.2 percent.[5]

4. The total wealth of the world's eighty richest persons equals the aggregate wealth of the poorest half, about 3.5 billion people. This means that if the latter group sold their wealth, they could just purchase that of these eighty individuals.[6]

5. If we look just at the United States, we see similar results. The rich are asset heavy, especially with respect to financial assets (those which yield income), and debt poor, while the opposite is true for those with the lowest incomes. In 2010, the richest 1 percent of households owned 47.4 percent of all common stock (excluding stock owned through pensions); the poorest 80 percent owned 3.5 percent. This suggests that the poorest 10 or 20 own a minuscule share of stock. The richest 1 percent also owned the lion's share of bonds, real estate, and unincorporated businesses. Debt, on the other hand, bears down most heavily on the poor. In 2010, for example, the poorest 40 percent of households had negative net worth, meaning that they owed more than they owned. Also in 2010, debt service payments made up 23.5 percent of total family income for the poorest 20 percent but just 9.4 percent for the richest 10 percent of families. A much higher fraction of poor families than rich ones were 60 or more days late paying their bills.[7]

With respect to all of these numbers, for at least the past 40 years, the distributions of wealth and income have become more unequal, nearly everywhere in the world.

The evidence on jobs is just as devastating as that on inequality. While economists and pundits babble on about all the good jobs that high tech is bringing, the truth is that most new jobs created don't have much cachet. The Bureau of Labor Statistics estimates that the ten occupations with the largest job growth between 2012 and 2022 will be personal care aides, registered nurses, retail salespersons, home health aides, food preparation and serving workers (including fast food), nursing assistants, secretaries and administrative assistants (excluding medical, legal, and executive), customer care representatives, janitors and cleaners, and construction laborers. Of these, nursing is the only obviously "good" job, and even here, conditions are rapidly being rationalized (cheapened) by cost-conscious managers.[8]

Today high-tech and low-tech jobs alike are shifted around the world by firms competing in the global marketplace, and this is going to continue into the indefinite future, as is the operation of the Babbage principle and Taylorism. And if you think most jobs in the United States leave a lot to be desired, then take a look at the world's poor countries: hundreds of thousands of young sex workers, camel jockeys, child factory laborers, adult sweatshop workers, and house servants. It is enough to say that in India, call center work is seen as a desirable job, and the call centers are filled with college graduates. In 2013, there were 202 million persons openly unemployed in the world.[9]

Although there have been strong environmental movements determined to clean up the world, they have not been very successful, given how much we now know about the impact of modern capitalist production on the environment. Poisoned food, power plant smog even in remote places like Big Bend National Park in Texas, scores of "Superfund" sites still mired in waste and filth and with no money in sight to restore them, global warming, mass extinction of species, cities so polluted that people have to stay indoors or wear masks, forests clear-cut of trees, the list goes on. It may be true that mother earth has an amazing capacity to restore herself, but it is a fair bet to think we do not have enough time left for her to do it before we are all of us dead or too sick to care.

The Future

If we don't change our ways, the future will be bleak. We have been traveling around the United States for the past fourteen years, observing how people work and live.[10] I shudder to think what my great grandchildren will see if they make the voyage of national discovery we have. One gigantic urban–suburban–exurban mess of traffic jams, strip malls, and concrete, marked by a bunker mentality and reality of the few versus the many (gated and guarded enclaves for the rich and hideous mass housing and prisons for the rest of us), all of us fearful of ever more devastating "natural" disasters. Don't laugh, these things are already here; we're not that far away from apocalypse.

The good news is that human beings are a resourceful species. If the many organized against the few and took things into our own hands, we could reinvent the world. There is no compelling reason why there couldn't be far greater equality, work worthy of human beings, and harmony between us and the natural world. I don't have any grand plan for change, but, at a minimum, I offer the following:

We have to bring capitalism to an end. The system has outlived whatever historical necessity it might have had. There is simply no way that capitalism can solve the problems we have seen everywhere in the country, much less solve these problems around the world, where they are many times more severe. Rosa Luxemburg, an impassioned critic of capitalism, put it this way: socialism or barbarism. We are well down the road toward barbarism.

If we reject capitalism, with what should we replace it? In the end, we will determine this in the context of our struggles to end a barbarous system and give birth to a new one. However, some things will be essential.

First, we will have to end the growth for growth's sake mentality dominating our own society. There is no need for output to grow willy-nilly without any sense of what production is appropriate and how the output is distributed. To limit growth, however, will require some national (and eventually international) planning. There is no reason why a national dialogue could not take place on priorities and needs and methods discovered for the implementation of what such dialogues conclude is required to be done. There is no reason why, especially given modern computer technology, that planning cannot be done democratically.

Second, much planning and decision-making can and should be done on as local a level as possible. If the Mormons in the West could plan their towns and their agriculture to meet local human needs, there is no reason why all towns cannot do this. What purpose does urban–suburban–exurban sprawl serve? Shouldn't it be eliminated? Shouldn't our living spaces encourage as much walking as possible? Shouldn't we have reliable and fast public transportation? Shouldn't we have good, efficient, and reasonably-sized housing for all? Why should homelessness and substandard housing coexist with 20,000 square feet mansions?

Third, our agriculture will have to be radically revamped, to end the sharp split between town and country evident around the world. Smaller-scale, locally-oriented, environmentally-sound, gardens-everywhere agriculture needs to replace, as much as possible, the large-scale, corporate farming that now dominates world agriculture. Consider that Cuba, despite terrible economic hardship caused by the collapse of the Soviet Union upon which it depended, achieved food independence in less than a generation after this collapse, and did so without super-mechanized and chemically-dependent agriculture.

Fourth, workers and communities must jointly manage as many of our workplaces as possible. Every worker should be trained to understand production and to manage complex modern technology. As much dangerous and menial work as possible should be mechanized out of existence, and that which remains should be shared out as much as possible. Alienating mass production assembly line-like work should be eliminated wherever possible, and production by coordinated work teams should be used instead. Swedish auto workers proved that this can be done.

Fifth, our education system should be scrapped and replaced with one in which the problems of inequality, work, and environment are made the center of study and in which the arts, both in terms of art as traditionally conceived and the mechanical arts, are taught to every student, not just in special subjects but integrated into all studies.

To those who say that such ideas are utopian and incapable of realization, I say this. Look around you. Isn't it truly utopian to believe that we can continue along the path we have been traveling for so long now and with such shameful and deadly results?

Notes

1 http://cheapmotelsandahotplate.org/2011/10/22/occupy-wall-street-and-the-celebrity-economists/
2 See Michael D. Yates, Naming the System: Inequality and Work in the Global Economy (New York: Monthly Review Press, 2003).
3 http://worldbank.org/en/topic/poverty/overview
4 Branko Milanovic, "Global income inequality: the past two centuries and implications for 21st century." http://ub.edu/histeco/pdf/milanovic.pdf
5 http://worldwatch.org/node/810#3
6 These data are from a recent report from Oxfam. The report can be downloaded at http://policy-practice.oxfam.org.uk/publications/wealth-having-it-all-and-wanting-more-338125
7 Data taken from Lawrence Mishel, et al., The State of Working America, 12th Edition (Ithaca, N.Y.: ILR Press, 2012), chapter 6, "Wealth."
8 http://bls.gov/emp/ep_table_104.htm
9 See http://ilo.org/global/research/global-reports/global-employment-trends/2014/WCMS_234107/lang—en/index.htm; Michael D. Yates, "Work is Hell," http://counter punch.org/2009/05/20/work-is-hell/
10 I wrote about the first six years of our travels in Michael D. Yates, Cheap Motels and a Hot Plate: An Economist's Travelogue (New York: Monthly Review Press, 2007).

4

MARKETS ARE THE PROBLEM, NOT THE SOLUTION

To hear mainstream economists talk, markets are the cure for whatever social ills we face. It might be true that, as in the case of rampant inequality, markets must be regulated. However, the idea that they must be eliminated wherever possible is met with scorn, and its proponents condemned to the crackpot fringe. Some on the left think that if we could end capitalism, we could somehow have a system of markets, where all economic outcomes are determined by the impersonal forces of supply and demand, and still have a cooperative socialist society.[1] This has always seemed nonsensical to me. Markets only work in the modern world if monetary incentives are in play, and for these to operate effectively, there must be private property. But once money inducements and private property exist, how can the negative social impacts of markets be avoided? They cannot. Markets and inequality go together.

A recent op-ed in the *New York Times* described the construction of "the mother of all luxury property developments" on Saadiyat Island in Abu Dhabi, complete with branches of famous museums and a university. We learn that:

Saadiyat's extraordinary offer to the buyers of its opulent villas is that they will be able to stroll to the Guggenheim Museum, the

Louvre and a new national museum partnered with the British Museum. A clutch of lustrous architects—Frank Gehry, Jean Nouvel, Zaha Hadid, Rafael Viñoly and Norman Foster—have been lured with princely sums to design these buildings. New York University . . . will join the museums when its satellite campus opens later this year.[2]

As might be expected, underlying this monument to excess is an army of laborers from Pakistan, India, Sri Lanka, Bangladesh, and Nepal. These desperate souls arrive heavily indebted to recruiters and those who pay their passage, only to be brutally exploited by sponsoring employers, who confiscate their passports. It is a system of semi-slave labor; workers are not free to leave, even if they have not been paid.

There has been no shortage of architects and other members of the "creative class"[3] willing to ignore the human misery and do the planning and designing, curate the museums, and administrate or teach in the university. The same has been true for buyers of the "opulent villas." One of the "lustrous architects" cited above, Zaha Hadid, also designed the 2022 World Cup soccer stadium in Qatar. In the past two years, nearly 1,000 south Asian workers have died building it. When asked to comment on these startling numbers, she said,

> I have nothing to do with the workers. I think that's an issue the government—if there's a problem—should pick up. Hopefully, these things will be resolved. . . . I'm not taking it lightly but I think it's for the government to look to take care of. It's not my duty as an architect to look at it. I cannot do anything about it because I have no power to do anything about it. I think it's a problem anywhere in the world. But, as I said, I think there are discrepancies all over the world.[4]

I have heard comments like Hadid's before. Billionaire George Soros says that his currency speculations are "amoral," even though they have wreaked havoc on the poorest people in entire countries.[5] It's not his fault governments haven't constrained his power to do whatever he wants with his cash. If he doesn't, someone else will.[6] Once at a faculty meeting, a colleague opposed our efforts to get the university to support the boycott of South Africa by divesting its stock holdings in companies that did business with the apartheid state. He said that there were problems everywhere, and we couldn't solve them all, so why single out South Africa. That those waging war against the brutally racist government had asked us to support them through a divestment campaign, that this was a problem we could address, hadn't entered his mind. On another occasion, I suggested to the dean, a physicist by training, that scientists had an obligation to consider the uses to which their researches might be put. He replied that this was none of a scientist's concern.

How is it possible that intelligent, well-educated people can ignore obvious human wretchedness, even when, as in the case of Ms. Hadid, it is right in front of them? Soros knows what he does is bad for society. My faculty colleague was a Jew who was quick to condemn anti-Semitism. Surely he must have seen the similarities between the inhuman treatment of Jews and that of black South Africans. My physicist dean must have been aware of the unease with which Einstein participated in the development of the atomic bomb, and his opposition to nuclear arms after the Second World War.

It is possible that Hadid, Soros, my co-worker, and the dean have uniquely flawed characters; perhaps they pathologically revel in the degradation of others. However, readers can probably think of like examples, and if we examine our own actions, no doubt we have at one time or another said similar things or at least thought them.

Maybe something different is at work. All of the transactions that will bring the Saadiyat Island venture to fruition occur in impersonal markets. They involve the transfer of money from buyers to sellers. And as the Romans said, *pecunia non olet*. Money has no smell. The plight of the workers is outside the purview of those who sell their architectural services or purchase the palatial homes; it is not a part of the market exchanges in which they are involved. These elite managers and consumers spend and receive cash in isolation from anything else. They cannot "smell" the suffering of those who toil so that their artistic conceptions and consumption dreams can be realized.

Our relationships with one another are often hidden behind the veil of the marketplace, covered by a shroud of money. We buy and consume goods and services without knowing who made them or under what conditions. Someone suffers so that we can have nice things, but the market obscures this. We are simply looking for the best deal; it is not our fault that exploitation lies beneath the surface of our buying and selling. We cannot be held responsible for this. Managers of corporations and political elites hire "creators," who in turn hire contractors, who then employ subcontractors, until finally those who sacrifice their bodies and minds are paid (sometimes) to do the hard labor. All along the line, markets and the money that makes them function seem to rule, coldly and impersonally, beyond anyone's control, or responsibility. Perhaps it is no wonder that Ms. Hadid spoke as she did.

Yet, not everyone wears blinders. For example, protests against conditions on Saadiyat Island have been made by artists and writers, through a coalition, Gulf Labor; recently some members occupied the Guggenheim Museum in Manhattan. They hope that their efforts will compel the museum to raise labor standards.[7] The Occupy Wall Street movement has fought to stop home evictions and to have student college debt forgiven. Chinese workers are demanding the right to have independent labor unions to end the factory conditions that have led workers to commit suicide.

Those who struggle against the victimization of workers are typically left-wing in their political outlook. What do they think is needed to create a society in which we have obligations for our fellow human beings, such that, as the Industrial Workers of the World say, an injury to one is an injury to all? Most confine themselves to political and economic agitations that might generate the freedom of those who labor to sell their capacity to work to the highest bidder, to form labor unions and to enjoy full political rights.

While these measures are necessary and admirable, they presume the continued existence of markets and the rule of money that accompanies it, the very things that provide cover for the horrors that define our daily labors. This acceptance of markets has been embraced recently even by self-proclaimed Marxists. Ben Kunkel, the writer, founder of the magazine n+1, and author of a book on radical political economy, said in a recent interview:

> So at least in theory, you could have a market economy where everybody receives the same income. It might not work for other reasons—because there would be, I suppose, no incentive at all to do a better job than someone else in terms of what you received in compensation—but at least in theory, there's no incompatibility between an absolute equality of income, and absolute freedom in terms of how that income's spent.[8]

Here we have a man of the left equating freedom with consuming and using equal income as an ultimate goal for a good society. By suggesting that we can leave markets intact as we fight to build a new world, Kunkel ignores the truth that market relationships, what Marx called the "cash nexus," are an integral part of capitalism. The labor market, in which our labor power is bought and sold as if it were a lump of coal or a piece of machinery, cannot be allowed to exist if we want to end exploitation. This market, like all others, is profoundly alienating, allowing us both to fail to grasp our subservience to the capitalists and to deny our complicity in a vicious and deadly system.[9] And as Marx scholar and economist Michael Lebowitz argues, we create ourselves as we produce and distribute society's output. If goods and services are made and dispensed through markets, the individualistic, self-serving behavior that these demand is bound to infiltrate our being. We will continue to find ourselves alienated from our labor, the products of our labor, and one another. We will be bound to make ourselves into human beings incapable of cooperative, collective productive relationships. Markets inevitably force us to act as individuals, responding to monetary incentives. We cannot liberate ourselves while maintaining a wage system and the selling of goods and services for a profit.[10]

Markets work well for the rich: those who rule Abu Dhabi, those who own the banks that finance the developments, those who sit on the boards of the elite museums and universities, all who own large amounts of capital. Over the past 40 years, markets have made the wealthy rich beyond their wildest dreams, with an ever-growing power to control markets and our lives.[11] What this means is that the liberal, social democratic struggles that met with some success in the past are not likely to be effective now. Sit-ins at museums and boycotts might provide temporary relief for the downtrodden, but not enough to matter much. Of course, some relief is better than none, but capital will always find ways to avoid doing what is contrary to its interests. The supply of exploitable labor is nearly limitless, and just when you think the degradation of men, women, and children has reached its nadir, new debasements are devised.[12]

We live in a world where the domination of markets is nearly total, in every country and in all parts of our lives. If humanity is somehow to move itself toward liberation, toward control over that which makes us human—the social nature of our labor—we must stop accepting half-measures. Higher wages, more equal incomes, better social services, even an end to the conditions under which men work on Saadiyat Island, won't be nearly enough if we keep buying and selling.

The precarious situation facing billions of the world's inhabitants every day demands our attention. There is always some awful problem that requires opposition. Yet, it is apparent, perhaps more than at any time since the industrial revolution, that the root cause of these problems is the capitalist system. The combination of the market veil and workplace exploitation has to be destroyed and replaced with a cooperative and collective mode of production and distribution. Therefore, whenever and wherever we can, it is incumbent upon us to name the system, to say forthrightly that capitalism is the cause of most of our misery. We must do this no matter the venue, whether the mainstream media, a classroom, a union meeting, or a training session. And we must bring this message to workers, peasants, students, everyone, whenever the opportunity presents itself.

Notes

1   For a good critique of this notion, see the section on "market socialism" in Harry Magdoff and Fred Magdoff, "Approaching Socialism," Monthly Review, 57/3 (July–August, 2005), http://monthlyreview.org/2005/07/01/approaching-socialism/

2   The op-ed is by Andrew Ross. It is at http://nytimes.com/2014/03/29/opinion/high-culture-and-hard-labor.html?emc=edit_th_20140329&nl=todaysheadlines&nlid=23341224

3   Richard Florida's term for the people who he claims are the key to revitalizing the economies of communities, cities, and nations. A website devoted to his book, The Rise of the Creative Class is at http://creativeclass.com/richard_florida/books/the_rise_of_the_creative_class

4   See http://theguardian.com/world/2014/feb/25/zaha-hadid-qatar-world-cup-migrant-worker-deaths

5   See http://baobabs.co.uk/words/soros.htm, for interesting quotes from Soros about what he does.

6   This is the implication of Soros's answers to questions posed to him on the television show 60 Minutes, December 20, 1998.

7   http://gulflabor.org/

8   http://salon.com/chromeo/article/tea_partys_absurd_socialism_obsession_an_actual_marxist_sounds_off/

9   For the best concise statement of the alienating nature of markets and the role of markets in capitalism, see Michael Heinrich, An Introduction to the Three Volumes of Karl Marx's Capital (New York: Monthly Review Press, 2012), http://monthlyreview.org/press/books/pb2884/

10   Michael Lebowitz, Beyond Capital: Marx's Political Economy of the Working Class, 2nd Edition (New York: Palgrave Macmillan, 2003).

11   See Michael D. Yates, "The Great Inequality," Monthly Review (March, 2012), available at http://monthlyreview.org/2012/03/01/the-great-inequality

12   See http://counterpunch.org/2009/05/20/work-is-hell/; https://monthlyreview.org/2011/11/01/the-global-reserve-army-of-labor-and-the-new-imperialism

5
WORK IS HELL

Imagine a triangle divided into slices. Let the topmost slices represent the wealthiest households. These are the ones whose members obtain most of their income from the assets they own. Those here who receive wages are often top corporate executives, and it would be fair to say, given that their counterparts in other countries make far less, that some considerable part of these earnings are, in fact, disguised profits. As we move down the triangle's slices, we come to the vast majority of households whose income derives from wages and who own few assets. The adults, and some children, in these households work for people in the upper slices. Thus, a fundamental inequality in all capitalist societies is that between those who own and those who do not, and between those who hire and those who sell their capacity to work. In somewhat crude Marxian terms, this is the divide between the rulers and the ruled, the capitalists and the workers. As we have seen, this inequality has been rising rapidly for at least 40 years in the United States, and in most parts of the world.

Ultimately, the maintenance of the uneven divide between those who labor and those who employ depends upon the ability of the owners of the mines, mills, offices, stores, and other enterprises to control the workers, to dictate how and when they perform their labors. The unequal power present in all capitalist workplaces affects working men, women, and children in multiple, typically negative ways. In a sense, all work is hell. However, there are degrees of misery, and I explore these in this and the next chapter. The importance of doing so lies in the fact that inequalities within the large and diverse working class can have significant impacts not just in life circumstances but in consciousness. While workers might be resentful of their employers' superior wealth, income, and power, they might also be hostile to their counterparts who earn either more or less than they do. If we consider those in the bottom slice of the triangle, we know that they often acquire money from government transfers such as public assistance, food stamps, disability payments, and other types of nonwage income. For a variety of reasons, including media, political, and religious propaganda, extremely poor households might be stigmatized even by those who are but one economic setback away from sinking to the bottom of the triangle.

Economists seldom say much about work. They talk about the supply of and the demand for labor, but they have little to say about the nature of the work we do. Like most commentators, they believe that modern economies will require ever more skilled work, which will be done in clean and quiet workplaces, by educated workers, who will share in decision-making with managerial facilitators.

We should disabuse ourselves of such notions. In the world today, the overwhelming majority of workers do hard and dangerous labor, risking the health of their bodies and minds every minute they toil.

The International Labor Organization (ILO), an agency of the United Nations, issues an annual report of its Global Employment Trends.[1] The report examines unemployment, poverty employment, and vulnerable employment. The unemployed are those not working but actively searching for a job. The working poor are those with positions that do not provide above a threshold amount of money. Two thresholds are used: $1.25 per day (in 2005 prices), which is "extreme poverty," and $2.00 per day, which is just "poverty." People in vulnerable employment are the self-employed (called in the report "own-account" workers) and unpaid but working family members in the household of the self-employed. In most of the world, vulnerable employment is what is known as casual work; the workers who do this do not have formal arrangements with an employer, such as a labor contract with stipulated wages. A man selling lottery tickets on a street corner, a woman hawking tamales in a parking lot, or a teenager offering rickshaw rides are examples of vulnerable employment. A child helping her mother sell the tamales is an example of an unpaid family member doing vulnerable work. In all countries, and especially in rich ones, not all self-employment is vulnerable. However, in all countries, but mostly in poor ones, the vast majority of the self-employed are poor and vulnerable.

The ILO estimates the number of people in each of the three categories —unemployed, working poor, vulnerably employed. Here are the data for 2013. There have been some improvements since the Great Recession but nothing especially dramatic. In much of the world, precarious employment, declines in the labor force participation rate (the ratio of the labor force to the population above a certain age) due to workers deciding to stop looking for work, and low wages remain the norm.

- Unemployment: 202 million (6.0 percent of a world labor force of about 3.4 billion. In 2009, at the bottom of the deep downturn, the rate was 7.1 percent of a world labor force of about 3.24 billion).
- Working Poor (using $2 per day as poverty threshold): 839 million, or about 38 percent of total world employment.
- Vulnerable employment: 48 percent of global employment of about 3.2 billion. This means approximately 1.5 billion persons in precarious working circumstances.

Two points must be made about these data. First, the number of unemployed might seem low to some readers, given the weak recovery most countries have experienced since 2009. However, in most of the world, open unemployment is not an option; there is no safety net of unemployment compensation and other social welfare programs. Unemployment means death, so people must find work, no matter how onerous the conditions. Second, the categories of working poor and vulnerable employment are partly overlapping. A self-employed person can be both vulnerable and poor, and he or she is counted in the labor force. However, an unpaid family member is, only in the statistical definition, vulnerable; he or she is not counted in the labor force. These are statistical quibbles. No matter how you look at the numbers, they are staggering indicators of what the world of work is really like.

To these gloomy numbers should be added another: there are, by ILO estimates, at least 168 million child laborers, age five to seventeen, in the world today. While this is a significant improvement since 2009, it still represents 11 percent of all children in this age bracket. The ILO classification of child workers is complex, but suffice it to say that 85 million children, a little more than half of these youthful toilers, are engaged in the worst forms of such labor: drug trafficking, armed conflict, slavery, sex work, and dangerous and debilitating occupations like construction, brick-making, and carpet-making.[2]

It is not uncommon for working children to live in the countryside or to have been forced from their rural homes, sometimes "leased" by their parents, and made to slave away in the cities.[3] The parents are peasants, two billion strong, and their future is increasingly precarious. Their connection to the land becomes more tenuous every year, and millions move to the cities, to become citizens of what Mike Davis calls the "planet of slums."[4] No amount of economic growth will absorb them into the traditional proletariat, much less better classes of work.

For nearly everyone in the world, work is hell. The sad truth is that the many have to be demeaned, worn out, injured, mentally and physically deformed, and all too often killed, on the job so that a few can be rich. I am aware that the statistics have been made worse by economic crisis and slow recovery. But should GDPs begin to steadily rise again and unemployment rates fall, will the world of work be transformed? Will we begin "slouching toward utopia," to use the pathetically inapt phrase of Berkeley economist, J. Bradford DeLong, who really believes that we are on the way toward a middle-class world of high-income and satisfied workers? I can promise you that we will not.

The devil, they say, is in the details. So, to give greater force to the data, I have added some concrete examples. I am sure that readers can add many of their own.

- Consider the automobile worker, Ben Hamper, who, in his book, *Rivethead*, describes a visit to the plant to see what his father does.[5] He says,

> We stood there for forty minutes or so, a miniature life-time, and the pattern never changed. Car, windshield. Car, windshield. Drudgery piled atop drudgery. Cigarette to cigarette. Decades rolling through the rafters, bones turning to dust, stubborn clocks gagging down flesh, another windshield, another cigarette, wars blinking on and off, thunderstorms muttering the alphabet, crows on power lines asleep or dead, that mechanical octopus squirming against nothing, nothing, nothingness.
>
> Hamper calls the modern automobile plants, pioneered by Toyota, gulags.

- Consider Mira, a child prostitute in Bombay, at age thirteen sent by her parents from her village in Nepal to work, they thought, as a domestic servant. There are at least 20,000 child prostitutes in Bombay, "displayed in row after row of zoo-like animal cages." We are told,

> When Mira, a sweet-faced virgin with golden brown skin, refused to have sex, she was dragged into a torture chamber in a dark alley used for "breaking in" new girls. She was locked in a narrow, windowless room without food or water. On the fourth day, when she had still refused to work, one of the madam's thugs, called a goonda, wrestled her to the floor and banged her head against the concrete until she passed out. When she awoke, she was naked; a rattan cane smeared with pureed red chili peppers had been shoved up her vagina. Later, she was raped by the goonda. "They torture you until you say yes," Mira recently recounted during an interview here. "Nobody hears your cries."[6]

- Consider Irfana, a Pakistani girl sold to the owner of a brick kiln at age six. Here is how she described her life:

My master bought, sold, and traded us like livestock, and
sometimes he shipped us great distances. The boys were
beaten frequently to make them work long hours. The girls
were often violated. My best friend got ill after she was raped,
and when she couldn't work, the master sold her to a friend
of his in a village a thousand kilometers away. Her family was
never told where she was sent, and they never saw her again.[7]

• Consider the lace maker, Mary Anne Walkley, immortalized by Karl
Marx in volume One of *Capital*. Mary Anne died 146 years ago,
but her story could be told today and not just of child workers like
Mira and Irfana, but by hundreds of thousands of garment workers
laboring in sweatshops every bit as bad as that of Ms. Walkley, and
not only in Pakistan and India but right here in the United States.
If you look up from the streets of Manhattan's Chinatown, you see
the steam from hundreds of sweatshops where today's Mary Anne
Walkleys work away their lives. Marx tells us that

> In the last week of June, 1863, all the London daily papers
> published a paragraph with the "sensational" heading, "Death
> from simple over-work." It dealt with the death of the milliner,
> Mary Anne Walkley, 20 years of age, employed in a highly
> respectable dressmaking establishment, exploited by a lady
> with the pleasant name of Elise. The old, oft-told story, was
> once more recounted. The girl worked, on an average, 16½
> hours, during the season often 30 hours, without a break,
> whilst her failing labor power was revived by occasional
> supplies of sherry, port, or coffee. It was just now the height
> of the season. It is necessary to conjure up in the twinkling
> of an eye the gorgeous dresses for the noble ladies bidden to
> the ball in honor of the newly-imported Princess of Wales.
> Mary Anne Walkley had worked without intermission for 26½
> hours, with 60 other girls, 30 in one room, that only afforded
> ⅓ of the cubic feet of air required for them. At night, they
> slept in pairs in one of the stifling holes into which the
> bedroom was divided by a partition of board. And this was

one of the best millinery establishments in London. Mary
Anne Walkley fell ill on the Friday, died on Sunday, without,
to the astonishment of Madame Elise, having previously
completed the work in hand . . .

- Consider cruise ship workers. Cruise ships usually register in
countries such as Liberia and are therefore immune to U.S. labor
law. The employees who do the most onerous work are invariably
people of color, typically from poor countries. Their pay is low, and
their hours are long. If they get severely injured on the job and need
hospital care, they are often forced to fly back to their home countries
for care, even if better care is available in the United States.

- Consider the restaurant worker, Mr. Zheng. In Manhattan,
restaurant workers often toil for upwards of 100 hours per week for
as little as $2.00 per hour. Here is how a reporter describes Mr.
Zheng's life:

> Three years after arriving in this country from the coastal
> province of Fujian [in China], Mr. Zheng, 35, is still working
> off a $30,000 debt to the smugglers who secured him passage
> on a series of ships. He can devote very little of his meager
> busboy's salary to rent, so he has 11 roommates. They share
> a studio bracketed by triple-tiered bunk beds, with a narrow
> passage like a gangplank between them. One bachelor
> household among two dozen others in a complex of three low-
> rise buildings on Allen Street, they split a rent of $650 a
> month, paying about $54 each.
>   Like the others, Mr. Zheng keeps his scant belongings in
> a plastic bag above his mattress, nailed beside the herbal-
> medicine pouches and girlie pictures that decorate his
> rectangle of a wall.[8]

- Consider the New York City cab driver, Koffee, an African living
in the city for 30 years. Here is an interview with him, conducted
by the newsletter, *Punching the Clock* (PTC):

PTC: So what kind of hours do you drive?

Koffee: Twelve hours, five to five.

PTC: Do you mind working a twelve-hour shift?

Koffee: That's how the industry, you know, they do it. In less than twelve hours you don't make nothing ... Sometimes you can work twelve hours and go home with about $20 in your pocket.

PTC: What do you do with your free time?

Koffee: Free time? I relax. With this job, after twelve hours you can't do nothing. It's a killing job. Sitting here driving for twelve hours. You get home, you are exhausted. You don't want to do anything anymore. I get home, I go to sleep. When I get up I just have time to get something to eat.

• Consider the voice of a worker unemployed during this nation's first great depression, in the 1870s. What he says could be said, with appropriate variations, by nearly anyone who has experienced the brutality of long-term unemployment, from the dust bowl farmers of the 1930s to the victims of the massive plant closings of the past two decades to the miserable jobless millions of the poorest countries of Africa, Asia, and Latin America. Just ask the next homeless person begging you for money.

Twelve months ago, left penniless by misfortune, I started from New York in search of employment. I am a mechanic, and am regarded as competent in my business. During this year I have traversed seventeen States and obtained in that time six weeks' work. I have faced starvation; been months at a time without a bed, when the thermometer was 30 degrees below zero. Last winter I slept in the woods, and while honestly seeking employment I have been two and three days without food. When, in God's name, I asked to keep body and soul together, I have been repulsed as a "tramp and vagabond."[9]

- Consider the farm laborers, everywhere among the lowest paid and most overworked. Bending over the crops, in terrible heat and cold, working alongside of their children, without enough to eat, like the coffee plantation workers who cannot afford to buy the crop they pick. In Mexico, just south of Arizona and California, here is what "free trade" has wrought:

> In the fields, a single portable bathroom might serve a whole crew of several hundred, with a metal drum on wheels providing the drinking water . . . Toddlers wander among the seated workers, some of them nursing on baby bottles and others, their faces smeared with dirt, chewing on the onions. A few sleep in the rows, or in little makeshift beds of blankets in the vegetable bins . . . As the morning sun illuminates the faces of the workers, it reveals dozens of young girls and boys. By rough count, perhaps a quarter of the workers here are anywhere from 6 or 7 years old to 15 or 16 . . . Honorina Ruiz is 6. She sits in front of a pile of green onions . . . She lines up eight or nine onions, straightening out their roots and tails. Then she knocks the dirt off, puts a rubber band around them and adds the bunch to those already in the box beside her. She's too shy to say more than her name, but she seems proud to be able to do what her brother Rigoberto, at 13, is very good at . . . These are Mexico's forgotten children . . .[10]

- Consider the workers in our packing houses, preparing meat for our tables. Before the advent of modern production technology, the very names of these workers conjure up a vision of hell: stockhandlers, knockers, shacklers, stickers, beheaders, hide removers, skinners, leg-breakers, foot-skinners, backers, rumpers, hide-droppers, butchers, gut-snatchers, gutters, splitters, and luggers. Then the work was done by European immigrants and African Americans. Today it is done by new arrivals from Latin America and Asia, but while the job titles have changed, the work is still dirty and dangerous:

> Beef, pork and poultry packers have been aggressively recruiting the most vulnerable of foreign workers to relocate

to the U.S. plains in exchange for $6-an-hour jobs in the country's most dangerous industry. Since permanence is hardly a requirement for these jobs, the concepts of promotion and significant salary increases have as much as disappeared. That as many as half of these new immigrants lack legal residence seems no obstacle to an industry now thriving on a docile, disempowered work force with an astronomical turnover.

Staggering illness and injury rates—36 per 100 workers in meat—and stress caused by difficult, repetitive work often means employment for just a few months before a worker quits or the company forces him/her off the job. (Government safety inspections have dropped 43 percent overall since 1994, because of budget cuts and an increasingly pro-business slant at the Occupational Safety and Health Administration.)[11]

• Consider Michael, who took a job as a hotel desk clerk after 32 years of college teaching. He says:

> I thought that at the hotel I would have the luxury of not worrying about what I was going to do tomorrow. But while it was true that I didn't have to prepare for the next day's work, it was today's work that took its toll. The job was tiring; I was on my feet all day. At the end of the day I was free, but too exhausted to do anything. I often fell asleep soon after opening a book, as early as seven in the evening. And on some days, especially Sunday, which was the worst day in terms of work intensity and customer complaints, I couldn't sleep at all. The computer keys I had punched all day kept going through my head in an endless loop, and conversations I had with irate guests kept bothering me. Monday morning would arrive and I had to be at work at seven, and I didn't catch up on sleep until about Wednesday evening. Teaching might have generated a lot of anxiety, but this was both physically and mentally debilitating. Thirty-two years of this would be unimaginable.[12]

• Consider the temporary clerical workers, Kimberly and Helen, two
of millions of such workers worldwide. Here is how they describe
their work:

> Minimal work. Boredom. And no challenging work. I'd much
> rather be fighting with a spreadsheet, trying to figure out how
> to set up a spreadsheet, rather than just entering in the
> numbers. A boss who treats you like a temp and is very much,
> like, always checking up on you or else totally ignoring you.
> Doesn't really remember your name. Says, "Oh, I'll just put
> this here. We'll wait till so-and-so gets back to work with it."
>   The isolation. The lack of benefits. The monotony. The
> underemployment. Your resources, your skills, your
> intelligence are not integrated. I mean, there's no change. So
> I guess just the hopelessness, just the stagnation. The fact that
> there's never any increase in cerebral activity. Even when they
> find out more about you, they still don't trust you to take on
> more. But the loneliness. It's really lonely. Eating lunch by
> yourself every single day. And no one ever asking you a
> personal question. Like the secretaries never, ever, ask, "Where
> are you from?" or "What have you been up to?"[13]

• Consider the college teacher, Beverly Peterson, who after spending
a good part of her life in school and earning a Ph.D., has become
a "gypsy prof," teaching here, there, and everywhere, under terrible
conditions for little money. About 70 percent of all college teachers
are now part-timers or full-timers with no chance of tenure, and
they earn about as little as $2,000 per course with no benefits. By
contrast, full-time teachers with tenure might earn eight or nine
times as much per class, with full benefits.

> Ever since she passed her comprehensive exams at the College
> of William and Mary in 1992, Beverly Peterson has searched
> for a full-time teaching post in American Studies. Three
> years, 121 letters of inquiry and two interviews later, she is
> still looking for a permanent position. "I'm so used to getting

rejection letters saying, 'You were one of 800 applicants for two positions,'" says the 44-year-old scholar, who once worked as a high school English teacher. So, while she waits to hear whether she will win a tenure-track job at Penn State, Peterson is taking the path followed by so many other newly minted Ph.D.s: combining two teaching jobs to make ends meet.

Peterson regularly commutes by car from her home in Smithfield, Va., to jobs at Thomas Nelson Community college in Hampton, 40 minutes away, and then to the College of William and Mary, an additional 40-minute ride. Peterson's travels take her across the James River drawbridge en route to the Thomas Nelson campus, and she takes a ferry back home from William and Mary. On the boat, she often works on lecture notes or reads class materials—most recently, a re-examination of Uncle Tom's Cabin. Her Chevrolet has some 97,000 miles on the odometer even though it is only four years old. Says Peterson, "I like my job, but I wish I could do it under easier circumstances."

- Consider the exceptional history teacher, Ira Solomon, teaching in East Saint Louis, Illinois, a town extraordinary in its poverty. This is what he tells Jonathan Kozol, author of Savage Inequalities:

> "This is not by any means the worst school in the city," he reports, as we are sitting in his classroom on the first floor of the school. "But our problems are severe. I don't even know where to begin. I have no materials with the exception of a single textbook given to each child. If I bring in anything else—books or tapes or magazines—I pay for it myself. The high school has no VCRs. They are such a crucial tool. So many good things run on public television. I can't make use of anything I see unless I can unhook my VCR and bring it into the school. The AV equipment in the building is so old that we are pressured not to use it . . ."
>
> "Of 33 children who begin the history classes in the standard track," he says, "more than a quarter have dropped

out by spring semester . . . I have four girls right now in my senior home room who are pregnant or have just had babies. When I ask them why this happens, I am told, 'Well, there's no reason not to have a baby. There's not much for me in public school.' The truth is, . . . [a] diploma from a ghetto high school doesn't count for much in the United States today . . . Ah, there's so much bitterness—unfairness—there, you know . . ."

"Very little education in the school would be considered academic in the suburbs. Maybe 10 to 15 percent of students are in truly academic programs. Of the 55 percent of the students who graduate, 20 percent may go to four-year colleges: something like 10 percent of any entering class. Another 10 to 20 percent may get some other kind of higher education. An equal number join the military . . ."

"Sometimes I worry that I'm starting to burn out. Still, I hate to miss a day. The department frequently can't find a substitute to come here, and my kids don't like me to be absent."[14]

- Consider two welfare mothes, Ursula and Joy, working hard to keep their families together but excluded from the official count of workers and reviled by more respectable society.

> Ursula: I used to feel downcast for being on welfare. It was something I felt low-rated about. It felt degrading. They want to know who is giving you this or who is helping to send your child to school. If I had to stop paying the water bill this month to keep them in school the next month, I would do that. But that's my business. I don't like them prying into what somebody may give me or who is paying something for me.

> Joy: When you are on public assistance, it's like you're going to pick up someone else's money that you didn't work for. You didn't make it yourself. When I got my first welfare check it felt odd, because I could compare it to receiving

my work check. I knew what it was like to have both. I used to hear people say, "Well, you are taking money from people that work and you are not working." It felt kind of funny to be a person on the other side this time. This is my first experience with welfare. Nobody in my household had ever been on public assistance but me. My mother worked for the government and so did my grandmother. I was the first person that ever needed welfare.

I don't like the people who work in the welfare offices. They are nasty to me. They have a bad attitude. They act real snooty and they really don't want to do the work. They act like the money is coming right out of their pockets. I figure, if I go in there with a nice attitude, because I know some people are nasty with them, too, then they will be different. But it doesn't help. They still are nasty.[15]

- Consider the following memorandum sent by a supervisor to a group of workers in a daycare center. Remember that these workers, all with considerable experience and many child-raising skills, are paid less than parking lot attendants:

> Now, more than ever, we as a business are under scrutiny by our clients. They will be watching us, and questioning us to reassure themselves that their children are safe and secure in our care. Your role is to do the best you can when it comes to customer service. They have made a choice as to where they want their child to be. And we need to reassure them that they have made the proper choice. We need to give them what they pay for every minute of the day. Parents and children must be greeted by name when they arrive in the morning and when they leave at the end of the day. You need to be working with the children, using your AM and PM lesson plans at the beginning and the end of the day. You are not permitted to sit on tables, chat with other staff people, or be cleaning or doing anything but interacting with the children . . . Remember, the customer always comes first and we always

need to do what's best for children . . . A pre-school classroom is a special place. It takes a special person to make great things happen for children. Always remember that we are tank fillers for the children. And that we owe it to the little people![16]

• Consider prisoner, Dino Navarrete, one of tens of thousands of prison workers now laboring in the "prison-industrial" complex, helping private businesses to make super profits. Could there be a more debased form of labor outside outright slavery? But as a matter of fact, this is a growth industry. The United States leads the world in number of prisoners, now approaching 1.5 million, and these convicts are overwhelmingly people of color.

Convicted kidnapper Dino Navarrete doesn't smile much as he surveys the sewing machines at Soledad prison's sprawling workshop. The short, stocky man with tattoos rippling his muscled forearms earns 45 cents an hour making blue work shirts in a medium-security prison near Monterey, California. After deductions, he earns about $60 for an entire month of nine-hour days.

"They put you on a machine and expect you to put out for them," says Navarrete. "Nobody wants to do that. These jobs are jokes to most inmates here." California long ago stopped claiming that prison labor rehabilitates inmates. Wardens just want to keep them occupied. If prisoners refuse to work, they are moved to disciplinary housing and lose canteen privileges. Most importantly, they lose "good time" credit that reduces their sentences.

Navarrete was surprised to learn that California has been exporting prison-made clothing to Asia. He and the other prisoners had no idea that California, along with Oregon, was doing exactly what the U.S. has been lambasting China for—exporting prison-made goods. "You might just as well call this slave labor, then," says Navarrete. "If they're selling it overseas, you know they're making money. Where's the money going to? It ain't going to us."[17]

- Consider Mike Lefevre, a "common" laborer. Here is what he said to Studs Terkel, author of the exceptional book, *Working*:

  > I'm a dying breed. A laborer. Strictly muscle work . . . pick it up, put it down. We handle between forty and fifty thousand pounds of steel a day. I know this is hard to believe—from four hundred pounds to three- and four-pound pieces. It's dying . . .
  >
  > It's hard to take pride in a bridge you're never gonna cross. In a door you're never gonna open. You're mass-producing things and you never see the end result. I worked for a trucker one time. And I got this tiny satisfaction when I loaded a truck. In a steel mill, forget it. You don't see where nothing goes.
  >
  > I got chewed out by my foreman once. He said, "Mike, you're a good worker but you have a bad attitude." My attitude is that I don't get excited about my job. I do my work but I don't say whoopee-doo. The day I get excited about my job is the day I go to a head shrinker. How are you gonna get excited about pullin' steel? How are you gonna get excited when you're tired and want to sit down?
  >
  > It's not just the work. Somebody built the pyramids. Somebody's going to build something. Pyramids, Empire State Building—these things just don't happen. There's hard work behind it. I would like to see a building, say, the Empire State, I would like to see on one side of it a foot-wide strip from top to bottom with the name of every bricklayer, every electrician, with all the names. So when a guy walked by, he could take his son and say, "See, that's me over there on the forty-fifth floor. I put the steel beam in." Picasso can point to a painting. What can I point to? A writer can point to a book. Everybody should have something to point to.[18]

- Consider finally this chorus of pained voices, again from *Working*:

  > For the many, there is a hardly concealed discontent. The blue-collar blues is no more bitterly sung than the white-collar

moan. "I'm a machine," says the spot welder. "I'm caged," says
the bank teller, and echoes the hotel clerk. "I'm a mule,"
says the steelworker. "A monkey can do what I do," says
the receptionist. "I'm less than a farm implement," says the
migrant worker. "I'm an object," says the high-fashion model.
Blue collar and white collar call upon the identical phrase: "I'm
a robot." "There is nothing to talk about," the young
accountant despairingly enunciates. It was some time ago that
John Henry sang, "A man ain't nothing but a man." The hard,
unromantic fact is: he died with his hammer in his hand, while
the machine pumped on. Nonetheless, he found immortality.
He is remembered.

Notes

1   Unless otherwise noted, the data in this chapter are from http://ilo.org/wcmsp5/groups/
    public/---dgreports/---dcomm/---publ/documents/publication/wcms_233953.pdf.
2   The data in this paragraph are from the ILO report, "Marking Progress against Child
    Labour," http://ilo.org/wcmsp5/groups/public/---ed_norm/---ipec/documents/publica
    tion/wcms_221513.pdf
3   See Jonathan Silvers, "Child Labor in Pakistan," The Atlantic, February 1996, available
    at http://theatlantic.com/magazine/archive/1996/02/child-labor-in-pakistan/304660/
4   Mike Davis, Planet of Slums (London: Verso, 2007).
5   Ben Hamper, Rivethead: Tales from the Assembly Line (New York: Grand Central
    Publishing,1992)
6   http://highroadforhumanrights.org/wp-content/uploads/2011/02/Indias-Shame-The-
    Nation2.pdf
7   Silvers, "Child Labor in Pakistan."
8   Deborah Sontag, "For Poor, Life 'Trapped in a Cage'" New York Times, October 6,
    1996, http://nytimes.com/1996/10/06/us/for-poor-life-trapped-in-a-cage.html
9   Charles H. Collins, From Highland Hills to an Emperor's Tomb (Cincinnati: R. Clarke
    & Company, 1886), 46.
10 David Bacon, Child Labor: The Hidden History of Mexico's Export Farms,"
    http://dbacon.igc.org/Mexico/03Onions.htm
11 Marc Cooper, "The Heartland's Raw Deal: How Meatpacking is Creating a New
    Immigrant Underclass," in Barbara A. Arrighi, Editor, Understanding Inequality: The
    Intersection of Race/ethnicity, Class, and Gender, 2nd Edition (Lanham, MD: Rowman
    & Littlefield Publishers, 2007).
12 Michael D. Yates, Cheap Motels and a Hot Plate: An Economist's Travelogue (New
    York: Monthly Review Press, 2007).
13 Kevin Daniel Henson, Just a Temp (Philadelphia: Temple University Press, 1996), 87.
14 Jonathan Kozol, Savage Inequalities: Children in America's Schools (New York: Harper
    Perennial, 1991).
15 Virginia E. Schein, Working from the Margins: Voices of Mothers in Poverty (Ithaca,
    N.Y.: ILR Press, 1995), 107.

16   Memorandum in possession of author.
17   Reese Erlich, "Prison Labor: Workin' for the Man," Covert Action Quarterly (Fall 1995), available at http://people.umass.edu/kastor/private/prison-labor.html
18   Studs Terkel, Working: People Talk About What They Do All Day and How They Feel About What They Do (New York: Pantheon Books, 1974).

6

THE INJURIES OF CLASS

Those who labor for others, especially under conditions in which they have little influence over the way in which the work is performed or the quality of the product, lose part of their humanity. We are all capable of both the conceptualization and execution of our work; this is one of the things that defines human beings. On the one hand, our capacity to transform nature opens up tremendous possibilities for building a world of both material abundance and great personal and collective fulfillment. But on the other hand, under conditions of capitalist control and exploitation, our capacities can never be realized. The grotesque rise in inequality has accompanied a growing alienation, a feeling that we are in cages, incapable of escape.

We live in a complex, divided society. We are divided by wealth, income, education, housing, race, gender, ethnicity, religion, and sexual orientation. These divisions are much discussed; in the past decade, there have been entire series in our major newspapers devoted to the growing income divide. And, "A search in the New York Times archives shows that between January 1, 2007 and January 1, 2014, there are 4,260 articles listed under the term 'income inequality.' Between January 1, 1977 and January 1, 2007, there are only 2,660 articles listed under this term."[1] The wealth-flaunting of today's rich has become a topic much reported on as well. As early as 2007, this was the subject of a Sunday *New York Times Magazine* article titled "At Their Service."[2]

What is seldom talked or written about is the most fundamental division, one at the center of our economic system, namely the divide of our society into a very large class of working men, women, and children, the working class; and a much smaller class of owners that employs the former, the capitalist class. These two great classes make the world go round, so to speak.

Workers and owners are fundamentally connected and antagonistic along a number of dimensions:

- It is through the labor of the working class that the goods and services necessary for our survival are produced.
- It is through the ownership of society's productive wealth (land, machines, factories, offices) that the owning class is able to compel that this labor be done. Workers must sell their capacity to work in order to gain access to this productive wealth, since no one can live without such access.
- In terms of society's "reproduction," the relationship between labor and capital is essential. So much of what we do presupposes the successful sale of labor power. Without the money from such a sale, nothing appears to exist.
- The essence of production in capitalism is the ceaseless accumulation of capital, the making of profits and the use of such profits to increase the capital at the owners' disposal. Competition among capitals both drives accumulation and is driven by it, in a relentless dance.
- However, to accumulate capital, employers must make sure that workers cannot claim possession of all they produce. This means that employers must strive for maximum control of the entire apparatus of production and any and all social forces and institutions that might interfere with this control (for example, the state, schools, and media). At all costs, workers must be prevented from getting the idea that they have rights to the output they make.

The organization of capital and labor in our society has negative effects on working people. Before examining these, we should note that the whole process of accumulation, beginning with the extraction of a surplus from the labor of the workers, is hidden from view, so that workers do not know or are confused about what is happening to the market, which embodies the forces of supply and demand, and effectively hides what transpires in the workplace. But other forces operate to obscure the truth too. One example is the public school system and the tireless promotion of individualism and nationalism at its core. The words of Peter McLaren and Ramin Farahmandpur quoted in Chapter 1 bear repeating:

> Today urban schools are adroitly organized around the same principles as factory production lines. According to [Jonathan] Kozol "rising test scores," "social promotion," "outcome-based objectives," "time management," "success for all," "authentic writing," "accountable talk," "active listening," and "zero noise" constitute part of the dominant discourse in public schools. Most urban public schools have adopted business and market "work related themes" and managerial concepts that have become part of the vocabulary used in classroom lessons and instruction. In the "market-driven classrooms," students "negotiate," "sign contracts," and take "ownership" of their own learning. In many classrooms, students can volunteer as the "pencil manager," "soap manager," "door manager," "line manager," "time manager," and "coat room manager." In some fourth-grade classrooms, teachers record student assignments and homework using "earning charts" . . . [Jonathan] Kozol writes that in the market-driven model of public education, teachers are viewed as "floor managers" in public schools, "whose job it is to pump some 'added-value' into undervalued children."[3]

Racism/sexism, imperialism, media propaganda, and repression further distort the social matrix and hide its class basis:

- Endless war magnifies and deepens nationalism and promotes both racism and male chauvinism. Wars send workers back to society badly damaged in mind and body.
- Imperialism does the same thing as war and often causes it.

- Constant Orwellian propaganda by the media, think tanks, politicians, and business leaders denies the class polarization of capitalist society. An important element of this misinformation campaign is the mythology surrounding the "free market" economy.
- When all else fails, naked violence ultimately serves to suppress class consciousness and sow seeds of doubt among workers who might otherwise be inclined to mutiny against the system.

Against this background, let us look at the "injuries of class." Consider first unemployment. The separation of workers from productive wealth creates the possibility that workers will be unemployed, unable to find a buyer for their labor power. In addition, we know from studying the history of capitalist economies that they periodically sink into recession or depression. Such crises are part of the nature of the system. In such circumstances, unemployment rises dramatically. Furthermore, capital is always searching the heavens for sunny skies (higher profits), and if it finds them somewhere other than where they are now, it shuts down one operation and opens another. Plant contractions and closings will therefore be regular occurrences.

What these things mean for working people is a pervasive sense of insecurity and fear that even what seems to be the most stable employment will "melt into air." Fear and insecurity not uncommonly produce two responses: a kind of joyless penury or a present-orientation that often takes the self-destructive forms of debt, drinking, and the like. In a recent essay, referring to the workers in the mining town in which I was born, I wrote:

> Mining towns in the United States were typically owned by the mining companies, and the companies exerted a near totalitarian control over the residents. They owned the houses, the only store (the infamous "company store"), all utilities, the schools, the library, everything. They had their own private police (the Coal and Iron Police in Pennsylvania) sanctioned by state law. The climate in such a town is one of perpetual insecurity and fear,

emotions compounded by the danger of the work in the mines
… It is difficult to overstate the power of fear and poverty in
shaping how working men and women think and act. Fear of losing
a job. Fear of not finding a job. Fear of being late with bill
payments. Fear of the boss's wrath. Fear your house might burn
down. Fear your kids will get hurt. I inherited these emotions.[4]

Should a person face an extended bout of unemployment or a plant
closing, the potential injuries of class multiply, as has been amply
demonstrated: suicide, homicide, heart attack, hypertension, cirrhosis
of the liver, arrest, imprisonment, mental illness.

The members of the owning class are almost always better situated
to withstand the storms of economic crisis or even unemployment, so
these are injuries that the system does not inflict on them. A few years
ago, Michael Gates Gill, a wealthy former advertising executive who
lost his job, was featured in the *New York Times* in connection with his
book, *How Starbucks Saved My Life: A Son of Privilege Learns to Live
Like Everyone Else*.[5] Gill gets a job in a Starbucks, and in it he learns
about ordinary people. By most accounts the book is not very good.
However, the author had connections, and not only managed to get it
published by a trade press but reviewed in our premier newspaper. The
chances of this happening to "everyone else" is as close to zero as you
can get. The stories of job losses are written in the litany of woes that
are an everyday reality for most people; such stories are anything but
exotic and receive almost no public attention.

Unemployment in our society is a constant threat to the employed
and a torment to those who cannot find work. To be unemployed is
almost to drop out of society; since to have no relation to the market is
not to exist.

I add here that those who do unpaid labor, especially homemakers,
must certainly experience something akin to that of the unemployed.
Their work is so devalued that an estimate of its value is not included
in the Gross Domestic Product. The unpaid labor of poor single women
with children is considered so worthless that they have been forced to
give it up and seek wage labor, often taking care of the children of others
while their own kids are attended haphazardly or not at all.

Workers comprise the subordinate class. They normally have to react to decisions made by others. Dependent upon employers, they are at the same time apprehensive of them, because employers hold the power to deny workers the life-sustaining connection to the means of production. Exploitation, dependence, and insecurity—in a system where workers are bombarded with the message that they and they alone make the decisions that determine their circumstances—make for a toxic brew, which when drunk often enough, creates a personality lacking in self-confidence, afraid to take chances, easily manipulated and shamed (on the bright side, these injuries have given rise to a massive "self-help" industry).

The very subordination of workers, combined with the market mechanism that ratifies and reinforces it, means that capitalist societies will display ineradicable inequalities in variables of great importance: wealth, income, schooling, health care, housing, child care, and so forth. What is more, the market will, absent powerful countervailing forces, not only reproduce inequalities but deepen them, as we have seen so clearly in the United States over the past 40 years. This inequality itself generates its own class injuries. As we saw in Chapter 2, all else being equal, the greater the inequality of income within a state, the higher the mortality rate. It appears that the psychological damage done to poor people as they contemplate the gap between themselves and those at the top of the income distribution has an independent effect on a wide variety of individual and social health outcomes. Everything we know about the correlation between health and other social indicators and income (a decent though not perfect proxy for class) tells us that working people will suffer in every way.

It has been said that the only thing worse than having a job is not having one. This may be true, but what does it say about work? Work in capitalism is a traumatic affair. We all have the capacity to conceptualize what we do before we do it. This capability, when applied to work, has allowed human beings to transform the world around them in profound ways: to invent tools and machines and to socially divide our labor so that the riches of the earth can be unlocked and a cornucopia of output produced. As we have done these things, we have also transformed ourselves, becoming ever more conscious of causes and effects and better able to understand the world. Put another way, our superior capacity to think and to do makes us human. It is integral to our being.

In capitalism, however, this human mastery of the physical world is reserved for only a few. The capacity to think and to do implies control, and control by workers cannot be contemplated by capitalists. In fact, the essence of management in capitalism is the monopolization of control by the owners, control especially of the labor process—the work—and its denial to those who labor.

We don't have space here to discuss all the various control tactics used by employers: the herding of workers into factories, the detailed division of labor, mechanization, Taylorism, personnel management, lean production—all of which deny workers their humanity, their capacity to conceptualize and carry out their plans, to actually "own" what they make. However, let us look at a sampling of jobs in modern America:

Auto workers: There are about 910,000 auto workers.[6] Not only are they facing rapidly rising insecurity, they are also confronted every day with a work regimen so Taylorized that they must work 57 of every 60 seconds. What must this be like? What does it do to mind and body? In this connection, it is instructive to recall from Chapter 5, Ben Hamper's book *Rivethead*, a startling account of working in auto plants. Hamper worked in an old plant, where the norm was about 45 seconds of work each minute. He eventually got a job in a new, "lean production" facility. He called it a "gulag." In her book, *On the Line at Subaru-Isuzu*, sociologist Laurie Graham tells us about her work routine in one of these gulags.[7] Below, I have skipped many of the steps, because I just want to give readers a sense of the work. Remember as you read it that the line is relentlessly moving while she is working:

1. Go to the car and take the token card off a wire on the front of the car.

2. Pick up the 2 VIN (vehicle identification number) plates from the embosser and check the plates to see that they have the same number.

3. Insert the token card into the token card reader.

4. While waiting for the computer output, break down the key kit for the car by pulling the 3 lock cylinders and the lock code from the bag.

5. Copy the vehicle control number and color number onto the appearance check sheet. . .

8. Lift the hood and put the hood jig in place so it will hold the hood open while installing the hood stay . . .

22. Rivet the large VIN plate to the left-hand center pillar.

23. Begin with step one on the next car.

This work is so intense that it is not possible to steal a break much less learn your workmate's job so that you can double-up, then rest while she does both jobs. Within six months of the plant's start-up, a majority of the workers had to wear wrist splints for incipient carpal tunnel. Necks and backs ache from bodies being twisted into unnatural positions for eight hours, or more, a day. Supervisors recommend exercises and suggest that workers who cannot deal with the pain are sissies.

What is true for auto workers is true for all who do this type of labor—whether it be in beef processing plants or on chicken disassembly lines where workers labor with slippery blood and gore on the floor and on their bodies. And where cuts lead to infections and disease.

Clerks: There are at least 15 million clerks of all types in the United States.[8] Many years ago I was on a television show with former secretary of labor Robert Reich. In response to my claim that a lot of the jobs being created were not all that desirable, he said that there were a lot of good jobs available, ones in which workers had a real say about their jobs (he was no doubt referring to the "quality circles" so popular then). One such job was that of "clerk." I blurted out in a loud and incredulous voice, CLERKS! I suggested that perhaps Mr. Reich had never noticed the splints on the wrists of many clerks, signs of epidemic carpal tunnel syndrome. Since that time, I have actually worked as a clerk, at the Lake Hotel in Yellowstone National Park. I describe the experience and what I learned in my book *Cheap Motels and Hot Plate: An Economist's Travelogue*. Clerks work long hours; they are on their feet all day; they take regular abuse from customers; they are exposed in full view of supervisors with no place to hide; they are accorded no respect (think about customers on cell phones in grocery lines); their pay is low; their benefits negligible. After a hard day at the front desk, I only wanted a few drinks and a warm bed. The stress level was extraordinary.

Restaurant Workers: There are more than 12 million of these, growing in number every year.[9] Next to personal care and service workers, those who prepare and serve our food are most likely to experience a "major depressive episode." Restaurant workers in Manhattan's Chinatown log as many as one hundred hours a week, for less than minimum wage. The pace of the work, the pressure of it, is unbelievable. Check out the arms and legs of a kitchen worker. They are full of cuts and burns. Substance abuse is widespread.

Secretaries, Administrative Assistants, and Office Support: These workers are more than 20 million strong.[10] They are poorly paid, many in sick buildings, stuck in badly designed chairs, staring at computer screens for hours, taking orders all day long (usually women from men), and often heavily Taylorized. Necks and shoulders ache; headaches are many. These workers, whose working conditions are satirized so skillfully on the television series *The Office*, have to contend with daily degradations, including all too prevalent sexual harassment.

Security Workers: At least 3 million men and women watch over others in prisons, malls, gated communities, in occupied Iraq, and on our city streets.[11] This is a type of work guaranteed to be stressful and to generate not only an extremely jaundiced and pejorative view of the rest of society but also an extreme, macho personality, prone to violence.

Custodial Workers: There are 4.3 million building and grounds
workers, many of them immigrants, keeping our buildings clean and
the grounds swept and manicured.[12] Often they are hired by
contractors who are themselves employed by the buildings' owners.
It has taken monumental efforts by the SEIU to organize some of
these exploited workers, who must often labor in close proximity to
dangerous cleaning fluids, solvents, and chemical fertilizers.

Medical Workers: There are nearly 12 million people laboring in
our hospitals, Urgicare centers, and nursing homes, as well as in
individual residences.[13] With the exception of those at the top,
including health care administrators and most of the physicians,
health care is a minefield of poor working conditions. Even nursing
has been degraded and deskilled so much that the nursing shortage
could be nearly filled simply by the return of disaffected nurses to
their profession. At the request of the California Nurses Association,
I spoke several years ago to nurses in four Texas cities. I heard many
tales of woe: sixteen-hour days, two weeks straight of twelve-hour
days, insane patient loads, constant cost-cutting that damages
patient health, demeaning treatment by administrators, etc.
Conditions only worsen as one goes down the health care occupation
ladder.

Work in today's exploitative society takes its toll on mind and body. It
saps our creativity, bores us to death, makes us anxious, encourages us
to be manipulative, alienates us in multiple ways (from co-workers, from
products, from ourselves), makes us party to the making of debased and
dangerous products, subjects us to arbitrary authority, makes us sick,
and injures us. I remember my dad saying, when emphysema (the result
of too many cigarettes, too much asbestos, and too much silica dust)
had sapped his health, that he hadn't expected retirement to be like this.
He and how many hundreds of millions of others? It is not the CEO
who suffers depression, hypertension, and heart attacks from being too
long on the job; it is instead the assembly line worker, the secretary, the
kitchen laborer. Those who cannot control their work hurt the most.
And with all of these injuries of class, I haven't even touched upon the

compound misery endured by black workers, Hispanic workers, women workers, gay workers, and workers without the proper national documents. And I have not described some of the worst types of labor: farm labor, domestic work, labor in recycling plants, and many others, which get truly demonic as we move outside the rich nations and into the poor ones. It is no wonder that people do not need much convincing to believe that happiness lies not in the workplace but in the shopping mall.

The daily debasement heaped upon working men and women breeds anger and rage. Often rage is turned inward and shows itself as depression, addiction, or suicide. Frequently it is directed against children, spouses, lovers, or against some great mass of "others," like immigrants, women, radical minorities, or gay people. But sometimes it is correctly aimed at the class enemy and takes the form of riots, sabotage, strikes, demonstrations, even revolution. And then the creativity bound and gagged for so long bursts forth as people try to take control of their labor and their lives. This is what I think of as the "miracle of class struggle."

I am not going to end this chapter with a reminder about how important it is to keep the struggles of the past fresh in the present, how it is necessary to educate the working class, of how it is essential to build a working-class movement and not just to organize workers into unions, about how there are any number of hopeful signs that such a movement can be built, of why we must always fan the flames of dissent and revolution. You have heard all this before.

Instead I am going to say something different. The injuries of class are deep and long lasting. The poor education that is the lot of most working-class children leaves scars that will not be healed by a picket line. The love lost when the factory-working father spent too much time in bars does not come back after a demonstration. I have been a radical, highly educated and articulate, but the fears and anxieties of my working-class parents are like indelible tattoos on my psyche. The dullness of mind and weariness of body produced by assembly line, store, and office do not go away after the union comes to town. The prisoner might be freed but the horror of the prison cell lives on.

Wilhelm Reich, the German psychoanalyst, was kicked out of the psychoanalytic society because he was a communist. Ironically he was also expelled from the Communist Party because he was a therapist who believed that the minds of working people, ravaged by the injuries of class, would have to be healed. It would take real effort to help workers regain their humanity. I think Reich was right. We ignore the injuries of class at our peril.

Notes

1 John Bellamy Foster and Michael D. Yates, "Thomas Piketty and the Crisis of Neoclassical Economics," Monthly Review (November 2014), 22.
2 Jonathan Dee, "At Their Service," New York Times Sunday Magazine, October 14, 2007, http://nytimes.com/2007/10/14/magazine/14portfolio-t.html. Be sure to click on the slideshow, which is titled "Catering to the Superrich."
3 Peter McLaren and Ramin Farahmandpur, "The Pedagogy of Oppression," Monthly Review (July–August, 2006).
4 Michael D. Yates, "Class: A Personal Story," Monthly Review (July–August 2006.)
5 Michael Gates Gill, How Starbucks Saved My Life: A Son of Privilege Learns to Live Like Everyone Else (New York: Gotham Books, 2007).
6 http://bls.gov/iag/tgs/iagauto.htm
7 Laurie Graham, On the Line at Subaru-Isuzu: The Japanese Model and the American Worker (Ithaca, N.Y.: ILR Press, 1995).
8 http://bls.gov/oes/current/oes_nat.htm#00-0000
9 Ibid.
10 Ibid.
11 Ibid.
12 Ibid.
13 Ibid.

7
IT'S STILL SLAVERY BY ANOTHER NAME

A book about inequality cannot ignore what has always been a fundamental divide in the United States, that between white and black. Several recent books have demonstrated with unique power that the development of the nation into a global economic power owed everything to the brutal and murderous exploitation of black slave labor. And as the long history, right to the present day, of police and vigilante violence against black people has shown with great clarity, the racial chasm lives on. A few black men and women have climbed into the 1 percent, and a sizeable African-American middle class now exists. But by every measure of social well-being, black Americans fare much worse than do their white counterparts. Just as for the economic, political, and social distance between capitalists and workers, so too the differential between blacks and whites for these same interconnected components of daily life continues because of the way our system is structured.

Right-wingers like Fox's Bill O'Reilly are fond of saying that whites don't have a monopoly on racism. Some black people hate whites, so they are racist too. Whites must stop being racist, but so must blacks. The implication of this way of thinking is that racism evens out in the end. It is seen as an individual defect, common to all of us.

The problem with this way of perceiving racism is that it ignores the larger social structures in which individual attitudes are shaped. In *Inequality and Power: The Economics of Class*, a book referred to frequently in Chapter 2, economist Eric Schutz suggests that as we make individual decisions, we, at the same time, make "social choices." These structure the larger society, which, in turn, conditions our individual decisions. Our political system is a case in point. The United States was founded as a nation whose prosperity depended heavily upon slavery, which was the dominant mode of production in the southern states and tightly integrated into northern capitalism. The slave trade, the production of important commodities, especially cotton, the textile industry, shipping, construction, the manufacture of agricultural implements, banking, finance, and many other economic activities were intimately tied to, indeed dependent upon, slavery.[1]

The slave economy was supported by a constellation of laws, enforced by violence, that maintained the entire oppressive system. Who enacted these laws? That is, were the "social choices" that allowed, defended, and maintained slavery made by everyone equally or were the choices of some weighted more heavily than those of others? It would take someone more obtuse even than Mr. O'Reilly to argue that in 1789 there was political equality in the United States. Slaves had no political power, and even among those who were not slaves, women could not vote, and, in many states, whites had to own property to cast a ballot. Blacks in the north were nominally free but subject to extreme race and class discrimination. So politics was dominated by white, male property owners, who shaped the government decisively to serve their interests, including the institution of slavery. And by the time slavery ended, inequalities of income and wealth had developed to the point that this white, male, and wealthy power was thoroughly entrenched and difficult to unseat. So what this elite wrought was also hard to change. Slavery ended, but the institutional setting in which it flourished did not.

Consider the conditions of black America at the end of the Civil War and especially after the end of Reconstruction in 1876. The slaves were freed but given no property, not even small plots of land so that they could feed their families. Without wealth or income, they had to fend for themselves. Federal soldiers protected them to a degree, but when the troops left, they fell victim once again to their white masters, who regained control of southern state governments and passed the Jim Crow laws that created a system of apartheid that dominated the south for nearly one hundred years. These states gave full sanction to white vigilantism, which stood ready to murder blacks who refused to succumb to white rule. Blacks were being lynched by white mobs into the 1960s. Through new laws that criminalized everyday activities, the white rulers of the south filled up the prisons with black men and women, and then contracted them out to white business owners, creating what a recent PBS documentary called "slavery by another name."[2]

If a group of people begin life with little income and no wealth, they are not likely to fare well economically. Modern research on economic mobility teaches us that it is not nearly as great in the land of opportunity as most people think. What matters most is how well off your parents are, mainly how much wealth they have. The children of poor parents are a lot less likely to end up rich than those whose parents are rich. Perhaps as much as 60 percent of the parents' income advantage is passed along to their children.[3] This means that a person's great-great-grandparents' wealth confers an advantage upon him or her today. By the same token, the poverty of your great-great-grandparents will haunt you now. Compound this inter-generational income and wealth effect with the impact of slavery and the "social choices" that whites made, nearly all of which created a society in which former slaves and their progeny were marginalized and considered barely human. Here is how I put it in something I once wrote:

> Imagine my own great-great-grandfather and suppose he had been a black slave in Mississippi. He would have been denied education, had his family destroyed, been worked nearly to death, suffered severe privation during the Civil War, and been considered less than human. Then in 1865 he would have been "freed," to fend for himself and whatever family he had. No job, no land, no schools, no nothing. For twelve short years, he might have had some protection provided by the federal government against the

murderous rage of white Southerners. But in 1877 even that ended, and afterward he would have been confronted with the full force of Jim Crow and the Ku Klux Klan. What chance would his children have had? How likely would they have been to catch up with their white overlords? Isn't zero the most likely probability? His grandchildren might have migrated north, but again with no wealth and not much schooling. His great-grandchildren would have lived through the Great Depression. How much property would they have been likely to accumulate? Finally, through the heroic struggle of my ancestors and my own generation, I would have seen the victories of the civil rights movement, the desegregation of the schools, the end of lynchings, and the opening up of a few decent jobs. I might have been an auto worker in Detroit for a dozen years, but then in the 1970s everything would have come crashing down again.[4]

Let's return to the argument that both blacks and whites are, to one degree or another, racist. If this is so, then, other things equal, the respective racisms should more or less cancel out, and no particular social outcomes would be expected to occur as a consequence of racism. That is, race wouldn't enter into the social choices Schutz writes about.

Can we put this notion of black racism and white racism canceling out to the test? Let's look at data that describe certain important economic and social outcomes: income, wealth, jobs, poverty, unemployment, housing, life expectancy, infant mortality, and imprisonment:

1. **Income:** In 1947, the median black family income was 51.1 percent of the white family income. In 2013, it was 57.3 percent. After the heroic struggles of the Civil Rights Movement and the enactment of numerous civil rights laws, this seems a small gain, and the 2013 ratio is lower than that of 1969, when it was 61.3 percent.[5]
2. **Wealth:** In 2010, the median net worth (all assets, including homes, minus all debts) of black households (a household is not necessarily a family) was $4,900, 5 percent of that of whites, for whom it was $97,000. If we confine our data to median net financial wealth (assets

include mutual funds, trusts, retirement and pension funds, etc.), in 2009, black households had $200, while whites had $36,100—a ratio of .0056. In 2009, nearly twice as many black households as white had zero or negative net worth (39.2 percent vs. 20.3 percent).[6]

3. **Wages and Jobs:** Black workers earn less than their white counterparts; black men, for example, earn less than three-quarters the wages of white men. The black–white earnings disparity is present at every level of schooling. Part of this is because blacks, no matter their level of schooling, are over-represented in jobs with relatively low wages and under-represented in higher-paying jobs. A report from the Economic Policy Institute tells us "The average of the annual wages of occupations in which black men are overrepresented is $37,005, compared with $50,333 in occupations in which they are underrepresented." Further, "A $10,000 increase in the average annual wage of an occupation is associated with a seven percentage point decrease in the proportion of black men in that occupation." Another part of the reason for the relatively low wages of blacks is that they earn less money within the same occupations. A summary of data collected by the Bureau of Labor Statistics shows that "in 2010, median usual weekly earnings of ... White men ($1,273) working full time in management, professional, and related occupations (the highest paying major occupation group) were well above the earnings of Black men ($957) in the same occupation group." For women, the numbers were $932 for whites and $812 for blacks. Racial wage discrepancies exist in every occupational category. If, instead of specific occupations, we look just at low-wage work, we find racial disparities, with 22.5 percent of all jobs held by whites in the United States in 2013 paid a wage that, for full-time, year-round work, would put a family of four below the poverty level of income. But for jobs held by black workers, this figure is 35.7 percent.[7]

4. **Poverty:** In 2013, the incidence of poverty for non-Hispanic whites was 9.6 percent; for blacks it was 27.2 percent. The percentage of blacks living at less than one-half of the poverty level was 12.2 percent, for non-Hispanic whites it was 4.3 percent. For black

children younger than six years old, the incidence of poverty was 42.3 percent; the rate for white children was 14.3 percent.[8]

5. **Unemployment:** The official unemployment rate almost always has been about twice as high for blacks as for whites. In March 2015, these rates were 10.1 percent and 4.7 percent respectively. Double-digit unemployment rates are more common than not for black workers, a condition that would be unacceptable if it were true for whites. In June 2014, the underemployment rate (which includes involuntary part-time workers and all those marginally attached to the labor force) was 9.8 percent for whites and 18.6 percent for blacks.[9]

6. **Housing:** Homes are the most important form of wealth for most households. In 2011, black and white homeownership rates were 46.9 and 76.8 percent, respectively. In addition, the current meltdown in housing prices has disproportionately hurt black homeowners. In connection with housing, it is useful to mention the recent study by the Manhattan Institute, which has received a great deal of media attention, that housing segregation has dramatically declined. The authors use a "dissimilarity index" as a measure of segregation and show that this has fallen. An Economic Policy Institute (EPI) evaluation of the study explains:

> They find a national dissimilarity (or segregation) rate of about 55 percent for African Americans—in other words, "only" 55 percent of African Americans would now have to move to neighborhoods with more non-blacks in order to evenly distribute the black population throughout all neighborhoods in their metropolitan areas. This is a substantial decline from the segregation level of about 80 percent in 1970.

Against the optimistic gloss that has been put on the Manhattan Institute analysis, the EPI authors make several salient points. First, a 55 percent segregation rate is nothing to brag about, and it will rise now that black homeowners in white neighborhoods have been experiencing so many foreclosures. Second, the dissimilarity index is a somewhat indirect measure of black and white interaction. By another measure, the typical black person lived in a neighborhood that was 40 percent white in 1940; today this has fallen to 35 percent. And even for the dissimilarity index, some of the decline is the result of an influx of Asians and Hispanics into black localities, while another part of it is the consequence of the greater economic mobility of the black middle class. Poor blacks have been left behind, stuck in almost totally segregated areas, without jobs as manufacturing left town and unable to follow jobs to the suburbs. "High poverty" neighborhoods are home to 40 percent of all poor blacks (only 15 percent of poor whites live in such neighborhoods).[10]

7. **Life Expectancies and Infant Mortality:** There is no reason to expect that, other things equal, one group of people in a country should exhibit different life expectancies and infant mortality rates than another. In 2010, blacks could expect to live four years less than whites. Infant mortality rates are more than double for black than for white women.[11]

8. **Prisons and the Criminal Justice System:** Here the racial divide is startling. In 2010, 2,226,800 persons were incarcerated in the United States, and an additional 4,887,900 were on probation or parole. Lawyer, writer, and civil rights activist Michelle Alexander calls what has happened to blacks here "mass incarceration," which functions much like Jim Crow: a "tightly networked system of laws, policies, customs, and institutions that operate collectively to ensure the subordinate status [of black Americans]." So, the United States has a criminal justice system population of over 7 million people. Nearly 40 percent of this population is black; more than triple the black share of the U.S. population. At every step in the criminal justice system—arrest, arraignment, legal representation, plea bargaining, jury selection, verdict, sentencing, chance for parole, prospects after imprisonment—blacks fare worse than whites.[12]

All of these things would lead us to reject the hypothesis that white and black racism offset one another. What is more, we would get the same results even if we conducted more sophisticated tests of this hypothesis. For example, black wages are lower than those for whites if we factor out schooling, age, occupation, industry, experience, region of the country, and whatever else we think influences wages. That is, if we look at two groups of workers equal in all respects (same schooling, experience, etc.), the black group will have a lower average wage than the white group. The same result would hold for whatever variable we considered—prison sentences, unemployment, life expectancies, and all the others mentioned above.

We are left with an inescapable conclusion. Having a black skin, in and of itself, is a grave economic and social disadvantage, while having a white skin confers considerable advantage. That this is true today, 150 years after the end of the Civil War, after three constitutional amendments, the great civil rights movement, a large number of civil rights laws, and lord knows how many college courses and sensitivity training sessions is testament to the power and tenacity of discriminatory social structures.

What might be done about black–white inequality? Some have argued that race-conscious remedies, such as affirmative action, are bound to be divisive and should be abandoned in favor of class-based relief. Some people I know objected strongly when a friend of mine suggested that anyone serious about racial disparities should campaign for the abolition of our prison system. While these persons knew that prisons are a key component of our discriminatory social structures, "abolish the prison system" would surely be an extremely unpopular plank in a radical movement's platform. It would have no chance and would just alienate whites and quite a few blacks from our cause. Better to fight for something like full employment through a public jobs program. This would have a wide appeal, and while it is race neutral, it would have a greater impact on black workers since they have much higher unemployment rates. A similar logic can be applied to national health insurance or low-cost public housing. The idea is to fight for things that unite the working class.

This perspective has a long history. After the historic 1963 March on Washington for Jobs and Freedom, at which Martin Luther King gave his "I Have a Dream" speech, key organizers of the civil rights movement began to plan how the movement might move beyond political freedom to economic rights. People like A. Philip Randolph,

Bayard Rustin and Martin Luther King Jr. understood that without ending poverty, achieving full employment, guaranteeing incomes, winning higher wages and providing good schools, national health care, and decent housing, the right to vote would not have much meaning. They also saw that these things would not happen without tremendous struggle, one that challenged not only the federal government but the basic structure of a capitalist economy. Their sensibility was democratic and socialist; it envisioned a society both egalitarian and controlled by the people themselves.

To provide the participants in this second civil rights movement with a document they could use to expand and provide a factual basis for the movement, a "Freedom Budget" was developed, showing both the need for radical economic changes but also their economic feasibility.[13] The "Freedom Budget" contains a section on the economic plight of black men, women, and children in the United States. It notes that the civil rights movement was led by black Americans fighting for an end to U.S. apartheid and for political equality with whites. But while they would be the primary beneficiaries of the destruction of Jim Crow, they would also, by making the nation more democratic and its people more equal, improve the quality of life for everyone. Similarly, the "Freedom Budget," while aimed at all poor people—black, white, brown, red and yellow— would benefit black people most. They had the highest unemployment rates, the greatest incidence of poverty, the most substandard housing, the lowest incomes, the poorest health, the least access to social services, and the most inferior education.

However, while those who wrote and promoted the Freedom Budget sought unity between whites and blacks, they also believed that, as with the struggle to end Jim Crow, black Americans would lead the battle for economic rights, and in the process make the nation more democratic and equal, improving the quality of life for everyone. They would make the country live up to its professed but seldom realized ideals. As the Freedom Budget put it "The Negro's greatest role on both of these fronts is not as a beneficiary, but rather as a galvanizing force. Out of his unique suffering, he has gone a long way toward awakening the American conscience with respect to civil rights and liberties. The debt which the whole nation owes him will be increased many times, as he helps to win the battle against unemployment and poverty and deprivation."[14]

While the Freedom Budget never gained much political traction, black people saw improvements in their lives in the aftermath of the Civil Rights Movement, notably a sharp decline in poverty. They won access to both better job opportunities and political offices. We now see many black faces on television news shows and in mainstream entertainment. Black CEOs, generals and presidential advisers no longer surprise us. We even have a black president. Yet despite undeniable progress, seemingly intractable racial disparities continue to exist. In the 50 years since the "Freedom Budget" was written, the United States has failed miserably to end poverty and deprivation. The black America that made the Civil Rights Movement and developed the "Freedom Budget" still suffers deplorable economic conditions.

It would be easy enough to construct a modern version of the Freedom Budget. In fact, historian Paul LeBlanc and I did just that in our book, *A Freedom Budget for All Americans: Recapturing the Promise of the Civil Rights Movement in the Struggle for Economic Justice Today.*[15] In it, we espouse several general principles that must underlie such a budget:

- Liberty and justice for all: equal rights and equal opportunities, with no exceptions.
- Deepening democracy: political, social and economic.
- A commitment to future generations.
- Comprehensive solutions: We reject tokenism and fragmented remedies.
- Harmony with global neighbors.

Then, we laid out concrete objectives consistent with the principles:

1. Full employment.
2. Adequate income for all who are employed.
3. A guaranteed minimum adequacy level of income for those who cannot or should not work.
4. Adequate and safe housing for all.

5. Health care for all.
6. Educational opportunity for all.
7. Secure and expanded transportation infrastructure.
8. Secure and expanded Social Security.
9. Food security for all.
10. A sustainable environment.
11. Cultural freedom and enrichment for all (arts, parks, sports, recreation).
12. Reduction in the inequality of income and wealth, to ensure the realization of these objectives.

Both the principles and the objectives reflect the working class unity point of view many on the left take today. However, this "unify the working class" strategy doesn't seem quite right to me. If it is true that the social choices made since the beginning of the United States have created racist social structures and if these have yet to be eradicated, it makes sense to have as part of a radical program a direct confrontation with these structures. If we had a full employment jobs program, how would it eliminate the gap between black and white wages, unless at the same time it was aimed disproportionately at black workers? If we don't aim to guarantee that blacks become leaders in our movements, then how will a full employment program or national healthcare or public housing be implemented so that they do not disproportionately benefit whites, who after all, hold most leadership positions in all movements, radical and not. Even if we were to make every element of the criminal justice system nondiscriminatory, how could we make sure that the enormous number of black men and women enmeshed in this system now will be able to extricate themselves from it and become full and equal citizens, unless we have race-specific programs to help them?

Given the extent and depth of white privilege, racial issues have to be addressed and attacked head on. There is no easy way out. The working class will never be unified unless we once and for all confront the institutional racism that surrounds us. Unity requires restitution for past and present damages. Nothing less will do. In our book, Paul LeBlanc and I make integral to our New Freedom Budget some additional suggestions, which call into question "class-only" politics. They reflect an understanding that racial attitudes are once again hardening, and from an already fairly unenlightened base, and the optimism felt by those who wanted a racially equal society has long ago vanished.

Political traction for A New Freedom Budget will require organization around community self-help efforts and political agitation demanding that the federal government begin to act in the interests of the people. With respect to the first, collective self-help measures, these can build cooperative entities inside the shell of capitalism and generate feelings of power, solidarity and self-confidence among participants. For example, the Occupy Wall Street (OWS) encampment in Manhattan's Zuccotti Park erected a small-scale society, providing themselves with food, sanitation, and housing while debating and implementing a form of democratic self-government. Remarkably, it did this in the face of severe police repression. In terms of the second kind of organization, political agitation, there are hundreds of examples, from the labor movement to anti-war struggles. Even OWS, which was accused of not having a political agenda, made many demands, including an end to police surveillance and brutality. History suggests, in fact, that collective self-help and political activism go hand in hand.

There is every reason to believe that black America can and must once again spearhead the fight for A New Freedom Budget. As the data above tell us, black men, women, and children are still the least of Americans. They have the most to gain from the achievement of the budget's goals, and their participation in and leadership of the drive to implement it would once again force the nation to confront the chasm between ideology and reality. And as past collective self-help and political movements make clear, black America has a history replete with concrete achievements. Without collective self-help, based upon the solidarity of necessity, black slaves could not have survived, much less create a culture that changed the world. This solidarity lasted through the long nightmare of Jim Crow and it forged the remarkable civil rights movement. Along with the demonstrations, marches, and confrontations with police, the civil rights movement saw collective self-help in practice.

In the 1960s, the Student Nonviolent Coordinating Committee's Mississippi Freedom Summer Project combined self-help and political action efforts. The voter registration drives were political confrontations with a vicious white state government, aimed not only at winning the right to vote in Mississippi but also to pressure the federal government to enact voting rights legislation. These voting drives were combined with Freedom Schools, in which students were taught traditional subjects like reading and mathematics, as well as black history and constitutional rights. Among black liberation efforts embracing a more nationalist path for struggle, the same kind of dynamic emerged. The Black Panther Party established "survival programs," such as the Free Breakfast for Children Program and a large number of free services such as

> "clothing distribution, classes on politics and economics, free medical clinics, lessons on self-defense and first aid, transportation to upstate prisons for family members of inmates, an emergency-response ambulance program, drug and alcohol rehabilitation, and testing for sickle-cell disease."

The Nation of Islam ran schools and day care services, operated a food distribution network, and established farms. Both groups in their "Ten Point Programs" also demanded that the federal government guarantee full employment, access to land, decent housing, good education, an end to police brutality in black communities, and an end to an unjust criminal justice system. Especially with the Black Panthers, community self-help activities were combined with active political struggles.[16]

Today, a large number of black organizations have been formed to combat police brutality and murder, the mass incarceration of black men and women, widespread poverty, and continued segregation and discrimination.[17] We must support these in whatever ways we can, but especially by being willing to honor black leadership. Black communities today have ready-made allies to help them win support for not just a New Freedom Budget but for a radical transformation of U.S. society. They could be joined by a growing population of oppressed minorities

—American Indians and recent immigrants from Mexico, Central and South America, South and Southeast Asia, China and the Middle East—to form a massive coalition leading all poor and deprived persons, as well as the rest of the working class, in building a society that guarantees, to all, lives free from want. Our political and economic elites caution patience and say that tremendous progress has been made in making opportunities available to all. This is simply not true. Most of our economic growth has been siphoned off by the very rich, while the lives of the majority of Americans become more insecure and less hopeful every day. We need immediate, radical change, and we must demand this right now, with black America in the lead.

Notes

1   Several recently published books show conclusively that slave production of cotton force-fed the rapid industrialization and commercialization of U.S. capitalism. Slave labor, under what Edward Baptist calls the "whipping machine," was enormously productive, much more so than wage labor, made so by brutality so extreme that, even in an age where violence has become almost routine, still has the power to shock. See Edward E. Baptist, The Half Has Never Been Told: Slavery and the Making of American Capitalism (New York: Basic Books, 2014); Sven Beckert, Empire of Cotton: A Global History (New York: Alfred A. Knopf, 2014).

2   You can watch this documentary at http://pbs.org/tpt/slavery-by-another-name/home/

3   Lawrence Mishel, et al., The State of Working America, 12th Edition (Ithaca, N.Y.: ILR Press, 2012), chapter 3: "Mobility").

4   Michael D. Yates, Cheap Motels and a Hot Plate: An Economist's Travelogue (New York: Monthly Review Press, 2007).

5   "Black median family income, as a share of white median family income, 1947–2013," http://www.stateofworkingamerica.org/charts/ratio-of-black-and-hispanic-to-white-median-family-income-1947-2010/.

6   Mishel, et al., 2012, chapter 6 ("Wealth").

7   Data in this paragraph are from http://bls.gov/news.release/wkyeng.t03.htm; http://epi.org/page/-/BriefingPaper288.pdf; and http://bls.gov/opub/ted/2011/ted_20110914.htm

8   Data in this paragraph are from U.S. Census Bureau, Income and Poverty in the United States: 2013 and http://stateofworkingamerica.org/chart/swa-poverty-figure-7d-poverty-rate-raceethnicity/

9   Data in this paragraph are from http://bls.gov/news.release/empsit.nr0.htm and http://stateofworkingamerica.org/chart/swa-jobs-figure-5n-underemployment-rate/.

10   The data in this paragraph are from http://stateofworkingamerica.org/chart/swa-wealth-figure-6j-homeownership-rate/; Mishel, et al., 2012, (chapter 6 ("Wealth"); and http://epi.org/publication/racial-segregation-continues-intensifies/

11   Data in this paragraph are from http://ecology.com/2013/04/01/us-life-expectancy-mortality-rates/, and http://cdc.gov/mmwr/preview/mmwrhtml/mm6205a6.htm

12 Quote and data in this paragraph are from Michelle Alexander, The New Jim Crow: Mass Incarceration in the Age of Colorblindness (New York: The New Press, 2012); http://bjs.gov/content/pub/pdf/cpus10.pdf; and "Lawyers, Jails, and the Law's Fake Bargains," Monthly Review, 53/02 (July–August 2001).

13 A. Philip Randolph Institute, "A Freedom Budget for All Americans: Budgeting Our Resources, 1966–1975 to Achieve Freedom from Want" (New York: A. Philip Randolph Institute, 1966).

14 Ibid.

15 Paul LeBlanc and Michael D. Yates, A Freedom Budget for All Americans: Recapturing the Promise of the Civil Rights Movement in the Struggle for Economic Justice Today (New York: Monthly Review Press, 2013).

16 Bruce Watson, Freedom Summer: The Savage Season of 1964 That Made Mississippi Burn and Made America a Democracy (New York: Penguin, 2010); on the programs of the Black Panther Party, see http://en.wikipedia.org/wiki/Black_Panther_Party# Survival_programs, and Joshua Bloom and Waldo E. Martin, Jr., Black Against Empire: The History and Politics of the Black Panther Party (Berkeley, C.A.: University of California Press, 2013); on the Nation of Islam's substantial economic plan based on collective self-help, see http://finalcall.com/artman/publish/Columns_4/article_6680. shtml.

17 See Danielle Allen and Cathy Cohen, "The new civil rights movement doesn't need an MLK," http://washingtonpost.com/opinions/the-new-civil-rights-movement/2015/ 04/10/e43d2caa-d8bb-11e4-ba28-f2a685dc7f89_story.html; Robin D. G. Kelley, "Why We Won't Wait," http://counterpunch.org/2014/11/25/75039/

8
THE GHOSTS OF KARL MARX
AND EDWARD ABBEY

This chapter was written in 2005, a little more than a year before the onset of the housing market crash that soon spawned the Great Recession. It has been edited, but it is the only chapter in this book that has not been updated. I wanted to show that the Great Inequality was well underway before the downturn, which of course worsened it, but did not cause it.

The first paragraph below says that we were on the road for 150 days. However, this was just one interlude in a continuing 14-year sojourn in the United States. In 2001, I quit work, began withdrawing funds from my pension, and we headed west from Pittsburgh. Since then we have lived in Amherst, Massachusetts; Manhattan; Silver Spring, Maryland; Miami Beach; Estes Park; Colorado; Boulder, Colorado; Tucson, Yellowstone National Park; Moab, Utah; Portland, Oregon; Ford City, Pennsylvania; and Kamuela, Hawaii. In between, we have spent well over 1,000 days in motels, seeing as much of the country as we can. Nothing has changed in the United States that contradicts the messages of this chapter. On the contrary, what is described here has gotten worse. Both inequality and environmental despoliation have risen dramatically.

My wife Karen and I were on the road, traveling around the United States, for 150 days. We left Portland, Oregon on April 30, 2004, and over the next five months, we drove about 9,000 miles, through 16 states. We visited 13 national parks, seven national monuments, and towns large and small. We walked on streets and hiked on trails; we talked to people; we read local newspapers and watched local television stations; we shopped in local markets; and we observed as much as we could the economics, politics, and ecology in the places we stayed. What follows are some of my impressions.

The ghosts of Karl Marx and Edward Abbey haunt the contemporary United States. Marx needs no introduction, but perhaps Abbey does. Edward Abbey was born in 1927 in Indiana, Pennsylvania, a small town about 30 miles from where I was born. He spent some of his youth on a hardscrabble farm in the nearby tiny village of Home, Pennsylvania, but he lived most of his adult life in the desert and canyon country of the Southwest. He was a novelist, essayist, poet, and a radical environmentalist. Among his best works are *Desert Solitaire*, an account of a year he spent as a park ranger at Arches National Monument (now a national park) in Moab, Utah, and *The Monkey Wrench Gang*, the novel that inspired a generation of militant environmentalists.

Marx argued that capitalist societies tended to exhibit poles of wealth and misery, with each pole tightly connected to the other. This prediction has been dismissed by mainstream thinkers, who argue that while there might have been some truth to it in capitalism's early years, the advanced capitalist countries have shown that all boats tend to rise on the tide of the system's incredible economic growth. However, if we look at the United States today, nearly 140 years after the onset of full-scale capitalism in the 1870s, we see that Marx's prediction still has a lot of life in it.

Marx was speaking of relative misery, that is, how those at the bottom compared to those at the top. Workers create profit by their labor, and the capitalists take this profit because they own the workplaces. If the workers are not organized, employers will squeeze more and more profit from their labor, and those who labor will become relatively worse off over time. Growing inequality is therefore the consequence of uncontested employer power. Other things being equal, there is no limit to rising inequality except the natural limits imposed by the inability of workers to minimally sustain themselves. Of course, if workers are organized, both at their workplaces and politically, they can and have placed social limits on the growth of inequality.

Today, the power of capital in the United States is more and more uncontested. Labor unions continue to hemorrhage members, and they exert a limited power politically. The state is more firmly in the hands of employers than it has been in 70 years. Property rights reign supreme in the law, and capital is pretty much free to do what it wants, whether that means firing workers trying to organize unions or moving operations to a low-wage venue in another country. Workers are becoming more insecure, without allies or organizations, and slowly but surely losing the social securities won by hard struggle many years ago.

The facts are readily available to show that relative misery is growing in the United States. We now have reasonably good data on the distribution of household income going back to 1913 (a household is a physical space in which people live, excluding institutions such as nursing homes and prisons). By 2000, the income share of the richest 1 percent of households was about 20 percent, its highest level since just before the Great Depression. It has been rising since the mid-1970s when it was just half this high. The rise in the share of the richest, 01 percent (a hundredth of the richest 1 percent) has risen even more dramatically, from well under 1 percent of total household income in the mid-1970s to a little over 3 percent today. Much the same can be said about the distribution of wealth—people's stock of assets as opposed to the yearly flows of income they receive. The richest 1 percent of households own a third of the nation's wealth, while the bottom 80 percent have just 16 percent, and this gap has been growing for at least two decades, although it diminished during the recent stock market crash.[1]

Both Marx and Abbey understood that capitalism devastates the environment. Abbey said, in reference to the environment, "Like my old man always says, capitalism sounds good in theory but it just doesn't work; look around you and see what it has done to our country. And what it is going to do to our country—if we let it."[2] Abbey documented in his essays and novels the destruction of the unique canyons, deserts, and mountains of the Southwest by the mining industry, agribusiness, urban sprawl, and the automobile. He had a good grasp of the fact that the growth at the heart of capitalism is incompatible with environmental health. He also understood that growth is not just a requirement of the economic system. It is also a deeply embedded part of capitalism's ideology. Senator Diane Feinstein, when she was mayor of San Francisco, said that she could not imagine the city not growing. Abbey had harsh words for this statement.[3]

The evidence of environmental destruction is as easy to come by as that for inequality. Consider just a few facts. More than 100 million persons in the United States live in urban areas where the air is officially classified by the Environmental Protection Agency as unsafe to breathe. In a world awash in toxic substances, the United States, with just 5 percent of the world's population, produces over 70 percent of the world's hazardous waste. Over a million children in the United States suffer from lead poisoning.[4]

Needless to say, inequality and environmental devastation are connected to one another.

Those at the bottom of the income distribution are bound to be those most affected by pollution, congestion, pesticides, and bad water. The rich can buy their way to relatively clean air and peaceful neighborhoods. Great inequality is deleterious to democracy and precludes any sense of common ground or need to develop social solutions to problems. Those at the bottom are so harried by the problems of daily life and so alienated from those at the top that they are likely simply to abstain from politics, leaving the well-to-do to make the government an agent of their will. Those at the bottom are forced into ways of living that are harmful to the environment, while those at the top see nature merely as something to be bought and sold.

I am an economist, so I am used to seeing the world in terms of data. But data alone do not satisfy most people. It is one thing to make the arguments I have just made, but it is another to have them resonate enough in people's minds to make them come to realize that the facts are part of their lives. To give the facts real bite, it is necessary to connect them to the lives of ordinary people. Perhaps I can do this by describing a few of the things we observed on our cross-country journey.

Signs of growing inequality are everywhere in the United States. Consider two especially stark indicators. First, there is an incredible and growing distance between the housing of the rich and the poor. The great increase in the incomes of the top 20 percent, and even more so the richest 5 and 1 percent, of families, combined with low mortgage rates, has driven up the price of housing, excluding those with even moderate incomes from buying anything but modest homes. The rich, however, are not deterred by high prices, and their high and growing incomes have allowed them to buy or to build ever-larger houses. For those at the bottom, there is no new public housing, and everywhere housing subsidies have declined and are under attack, so they must live where they can. What we end up with is a kind of housing apartheid.

No matter where you go, the well-to-do have isolated their living spaces from everyone else's. Either they are living in gated or otherwise guarded communities or they are buying enormous tracts of land and building bigger and bigger mansions on them, sometimes complete with private roads and security guards. Often the growing political power of those with money allows them to obtain, through the lobbying of real estate and banking interests, large tax breaks for "developing" the land. Sometimes, as was the case in the Pearl District of Portland, Oregon, tax breaks were given not only to the developers who converted warehouses into swank condominiums but to the buyers as well.

Consider the towns of Florence, Oregon and Santa Fe, New Mexico. Florence is on the central Oregon coast, the northern gateway town to the fifty-mile stretch of sand dunes that hug the coast south to Coos Bay. Florence used to be a small fishing town, and there are still working boats at the dock on the Siuslaw River in the Old Town, not far from the gorgeous art deco bridge on Highway 101, built by the Works Progress Administration during the Great Depression. Like a lot of small working-class towns, Florence has a nice feel to it, easy-going and friendly. But the surrounding area is growing, attracting people with more money who think they will enjoy the slower pace of life. A drive to the beach next to the north jetty where the river meets the Pacific Ocean takes you past several gated communities. I was struck by these; I wondered why gates were needed in such a place. But income disparity is growing, as evidenced by the recent construction of a casino, a sure sign that good jobs are rare, and no doubt the wealthier newcomers feel safer behind gates. I note in passing that we also saw a gated community in the dirt poor and dusty southern California desert town of Twentynine Palms.

Santa Fe will be more familiar to readers. Much larger than Florence, it is the state capital of New Mexico, with a reputation for sophistication that attracts thousands of visitors annually to its opera, Indian market, and museums. It is the second largest art market in the United States; only New York City's is larger. Along Canyon Road, there are more than one hundred art dealers. In the downtown, there are several excellent art museums, including one dedicated to the works of Georgia O'Keefe, many fine restaurants, and at least a half-dozen smart hotels. The town's geographical setting is glorious, with easily reachable mountains rising to over 13,000 feet to the north and east. Much of the year the weather is warm and sunny.

Not many people live in Santa Fe's downtown; we could not find a drugstore or a chain grocery store there. But if you take a hike in any of the surrounding hills, houses can be seen that boggle the mind. One morning we began a hike at St. John's College, located east of downtown. This college is the sister school to the one of the same name in Annapolis, Maryland; both are famous for their focus on a "Great Books" curriculum. We parked in a college lot and after crossing two arroyos, we headed up a hill toward Atalaya Mountain. We came to a private road that entered a very posh gated community, filled with large adobe-style houses, probably priced at one million dollars or more. As we ascended the mountain, we came upon isolated homes, each more spectacular than the one before. These were gigantic adobe structures, containing upwards of 10,000 square feet of living space plus various outbuildings, gardens, stables, and swimming pools. As we discovered in our travels, these estates are often not occupied year round but are just one of several homes of the owners. And as a perusal of the real estate ads in the *New York Times Magazine* shows, such estates can cost as much as ten million dollars.

The southern entrance to Santa Fe is Cerillos Road, a congested and ugly ten-mile stretch of strip malls, motels, businesses, and retail stores. It is on the streets behind this road that one encounters the houses and apartments of the poorly paid workers who service tourists in restaurants and downtown hotels and shops. We learned this from a clerk in a bookstore who told us that many service workers earned the minimum wage or slightly above and found it difficult to find adequate housing in Santa Fe. Still poorer housing can be found in the predominantly Indian villages close to the town. Although we did not observe this in Santa Fe, it is not uncommon to see entire families living in the cheapest motels. Unable to find housing, these migrants seeking work hole up in motels hoping for something better. I had thought that these people must be mainly immigrants or displaced manufacturing workers. However, a recent article in the *Washington Post* described a new phenomenon: highly skilled but displaced information technology workers living in motels, often with their families, while they completed a temporary job assignment. One worker complained that the $58 per day he was paying for a motel room was eating deeply into his wage, much as a city cab driver might worry about meeting his daily cab leasing and gas expenditures or a criminal gang member might wonder how he was going to meet his weekly quota.[5]

Those upper-income households that are not rich but still have considerable income are moving to what *New York Times* columnist David Brooks calls the "exurbs."[6] Santa Fe does not really have exurbs, that is, areas removed even from the suburbs and not necessarily connected to a city. Such regions are, contrary to Brooks' panegyric to them as incubators of new technology, rather lifeless places of expensive tract housing sitting on treeless lots and without much in the way of social amenities. Employers are building office complexes and other workplaces in the exurbs, far away from the higher taxes and unions of the cities or even the older suburbs. Exurbs can be seen all around the country. We saw them near Albuquerque, New Mexico, sprawling endlessly away from the city center, as well as along Interstate 5 in Oregon and California.

The second striking feature of inequality in the United States is its racial and ethnic face. While there are exceptions, in the United States today poor means black or brown and rich means white. This is something that I am certain most white people fail to notice. When we lived in Portland and pointed out to people that there was no diversity in the city, they would say, "Well, I never thought of that." We noticed right away that the only people of color in every upper-income neighborhood were the Mexican gardeners and construction laborers.

Before I give some examples of the racial and ethnic divide overlapping growing inequality, let us look at some numbers. Median family income (in 2003 dollars) for whites in 2002 was $55,885, but for blacks it was $34,293 and for Hispanics $34,968. While 20.4 percent of white workers earned a wage that would not support a family of four at the poverty level of income, for black workers it was 30.4 percent and for Hispanics 39.8 percent. Since the mid-1970s, the average unemployment rate for whites is a little over 5 percent. For blacks it is over 13 percent, and for Hispanics it is more than 9 percent. These unemployment differences understate the true differences because relatively more blacks and Hispanics are out of the labor force than is true for whites. For example, blacks comprise only a bit more than 11 percent of all workers, but they represent nearly half of the 2.2 million persons in our prisons and jails. The rapid increase in the rate of black imprisonment over the past three decades has had a devastating impact on the integrity of black communities. If we look at the wealth data, the racial gap is startling. In 2001, the median net worth (assets minus debts) of black households was $10,700, compared to $106,400 for white households. This includes all wealth, of which houses are a major component for all but the wealthy. If we include only financial wealth (stocks, bonds, and cash), median black wealth is a mere $1,100; for whites it is $42,100. Thirty-one percent of black households have zero or negative net wealth, while only 14 percent of white households do. Data for Hispanic household wealth is not available, but it is surely much lower than that for whites.

The racial and ethnic divide can be seen everywhere and in virtually all aspects of daily life. The fine houses we saw and the gated communities were invariably inhabited by whites. The people we saw living in motels were persons of color. The shabbier grocery stores we visited were mostly frequented by people of color, but if we went to an upscale market such as Whole Foods, New Frontiers, or Wild Oats, the clientele was typically white. We often shopped in ethnic markets, and unlike places such as Manhattan where these markets attract a heterogeneous group of shoppers, in towns like Santa Fe, Taos, or Flagstaff, we might be the only white persons in the store. In downtown areas, Hispanics, American Indians, and blacks commingle with the tourists (on the streets at least; if there is a museum exhibit or a symphony concert, the audience will be overwhelmingly white), but the fancier suburbs and exurbs are mostly white preserves.

The racial and ethnic divide becomes a chasm when it comes to the work people do. It is a safe bet that if there is a low-wage, low-status job, a person of color will be working at it. Throughout the West, we saw prisoners doing various types of roadwork, under the supervision of armed guards. A white worker here was as rare as rain in Death Valley. We stayed in nearly thirty motels, several for a week and one for twenty-two days. We saw hundreds of desk clerks, maintenance personnel, and housekeepers. It was very much more likely that a desk clerk, the person who first meets the guest, would be white than a housekeeper. In fact, in the five months we traveled, we met exactly one white housekeeper (not counting the national parks, where white Eastern European young people without English are recruited by the parks' concessionaires and then, often against their wishes, set to cleaning rooms). Nearly all the rest were from Latin America. All were women. Most spoke little or no English, and many may have been in the United States without documents. It was not uncommon for them to bring their small children to work and for a co-worker to watch the kids when she was not working.

We had an encounter with the one white housekeeper we met. We were staying at a motel in an isolated, small, and uniformly white town in Utah. We were there for seven days, and we noticed that our room was not being cleaned. The bed was made but nothing else was done. We are sensitive to what housekeepers have to put up with; we always leave a gratuity, and we make sure that the room is tidy and uncluttered before we leave each morning. But we felt that a room ought to be cleaned, so after three days of living in a dirty room, we asked the housekeeper if she had cleaned our room, and when she said yes, we invited her in to show her that it had not been cleaned. Then she said, "Oh, we don't do cleaning." We were taken aback and asked her why not. She said that she did not like to interfere with people's belongings. We said that we had put all our things away, even repacking our toiletries, so there was nothing to interfere with. In a huff, she said she would return to clean. She did, making a halfhearted effort to clean the floor and sink. We noticed that she was dressed in an inappropriate manner for cleaning rooms, wearing a dressy long-sleeve blouse and pants. She was so angry that she complained about us to the owners, a remarkable thing since the owners were apologetic and told us that they were always telling the housekeepers that they had to clean the rooms. What was going on here? Did this event have something to do with race? This was a white town; Hispanic immigrants hadn't arrived here yet. So, only local white women could be recruited. They would do the work, no doubt out of economic necessity. But it was clear that they considered this labor beneath them. It was not "white" work, and they would not demean themselves by working hard like their darker-skinned sisters. And unlike the Hispanic housekeepers we met everywhere else, these white women could not be easily replaced, because there was not a ready pool of surplus laborers to take their place. White skin privilege runs deep, and it thoroughly divides the working class.

What was true in the motels was also true in restaurants. Where it is possible to recruit them, as in our national parks, waiters are more likely to be white, while kitchen dishwashers and cooks are seldom white. Laundromat attendants, convenience store and gas station workers, grocery store clerks, baggers, and stockers, retail store workers, gardeners, non-union construction laborers, farm workers—whites are seldom seen in these jobs. In the West, Hispanics, American Indians, and blacks do the dirty work. And, they live in the worst housing, are most likely to be homeless, and inhabit most of the prison cells.

We ended our journey in Miami Beach, Florida. This is a good place to observe both inequality and the racial divide. We often walked down the beach to the pier at the southern end of town. Here we watched the giant container ships delivering cargo to the port at Miami and carrying cargo out to the far corners of the earth. We also observed the huge cruise ships taking tourists to exotic places. The travelers waved to the people on the pier, and at night the ships looked like decorated mansions as they made their way out to sea. However, underlying this tranquil scene is a reality of harsh and dangerous work. These ships usually register in countries such as Liberia and are therefore immune to U.S. labor law. The employees who do the most onerous work are invariably people of color, typically from poor countries. Their pay is low, and their hours are long. If they get severely injured on the job and need hospital care, they are often forced to fly back to their home countries for care even if better care is available in the United States. One worker from a Caribbean nation slipped on a kitchen floor while carrying a large pot of oil. The oil severely burned his leg and foot. He was taken out of a hospital in Anchorage, Alaska and forced to take several flights home. He called his mother in desperation and managed at a stopover in Miami to contact a lawyer his mother knew of through a friend. This lawyer managed to get him care in Miami, and then sued the shipping company. The company retaliated by contacting the immigration authorities who promptly deported the man.[7]

"Development" and "growth" are the watchwords of capitalism in the United States. Environmental protection is an afterthought; when this conflicts with growth, growth wins. Two things you can't miss if you drive around the country are urban-suburban-exurban sprawl, heavily subsidized by the government, and private use of public lands. Examples are almost too numerous to mention. Los Angeles is everybody's poster child for sprawl. It is quite an experience to drive in and around this city, seeing everywhere clogged highways and tangles of freeway entrance and exit ramps, close by endless unsightly housing developments, the whole mess made possible by a hundred years of publicly-financed dam-building and river-ruining. The city and its suburbs extend far into the deserts north and south. Once beyond these there are towns and development everywhere, all suffering from smog and industrial pollution. One hundred and fifty miles southeast of Los Angeles, just outside Twentynine Palms, is the relatively pristine desert of Joshua Tree

National Park. From the top of Keys View (the highest point in the park accessible by car), the resort town of Palm Springs, with its hundred golf courses shamelessly wasting water, is visible. Visible too is the brown Los Angeles smog snaking its way through a mountain pass, corrupting even this special place. The insanity of a megalopolis in the desert is further brought home by something else which can be seen—the San Andreas Fault.

Growth run wild can also be witnessed in Albuquerque, New Mexico and Denver, Colorado. Albuquerque's population has quadrupled, to about 800,000, since the 1950s, and it now spreads out interminably from the intersection of Interstates 15 and 40. There are now nineteen Albuquerque freeway exits, and residents think still more are needed to accommodate the ceaseless traffic. There is no way to go from one place to another in this city without getting on an interstate highway. What seems like an infinity of suburbs and exurbs crowd out the desert, filled with developments of cheaply-built but expensive homes on treeless lots baking in the sun and running now almost all the way to Santa Fe, sixty miles north. Perhaps hidden in one of the nondescript industrial parks that pockmark the landscape in the exurbs are the scientists developing nanotechnology about whom David Brooks gushes when he writes of the exurbs as an exciting new frontier. But even technological advance does not seem worth the social cost of such land-destroying, water-wasting, and air-polluting ugliness.

Denver, a few hundred miles north of Albuquerque on Interstate 15, is another mess of relentless traffic and highway building. North of the city, farmlands are being rapidly converted into faceless housing developments. The juxtaposition of farms and housing tracts, again on lots without trees and with houses so similar that it must sometimes be difficult to find your own on a dark night, is difficult to absorb. However, it will not be long before the farms have disappeared altogether and Denver goes on forever. The logic of capitalism, which today is nearly as unfettered as it was in the 1920s, dictates that land will be put to whatever use can generate the most profits. Economically-strapped farmers will sell their fields to developers who will make a fortune, shared with construction companies and politicians on the take, building new exurbs. Governments will accommodate them with new zoning laws, more highways, and subsidized industrial parks.

In theory the public lands of the United States belong to all the people. In reality, many public lands might as well be private property, and much public land is always under threat of being sold to private developers. Throughout the West, cattle graze on public lands irrigated with public water and in the process ruin the terrain and pollute rivers and streams in an extraordinarily socially inefficient operation. Communication towers pollute the peaks of publicly-owned mountains; high above Albuquerque near Sandia Peak there is a mass of such towers called without irony by the government a "steel forest." Even in the national parks, cell phone towers are being constructed so that the tourists can chat with their friends and tell them what wonderful sights they are seeing. Signs in our national forests proclaim that these are lands of "many uses." Odd that so many of these uses are commercial. Roads are rapidly being built in these forests so that lumber companies may soon log out the trees. Today mines and wells can be dug from outside public lands at an angle going into them, and this is fine by the government. The running of most of the national parks has from their beginnings been the province of private enterprise. The Xanterra Corporation (formerly one of the "big five" sugar overlords of Hawaii) today has the concessions at several parks and actually owns part of the water rights at Death Valley and property rights in the historic buildings of Grand Canyon National Park. We have not even been able to prevent the use of snowmobiles (promoted heavily by businesses in West Yellowstone and other gateway towns) in Yellowstone National Park, despite the obvious damage they do to the environment. Gate attendants at the park now have to wear masks to protect themselves from the pollution caused by the machines.[8]

The usurpation of public lands by private interests is very likely greater at state and local levels where business can exert enormous influence on public officials and where the latter are more willing subjects of influence peddling. Virginia Key is an oasis of natural beauty and tranquility offshore from but part of the crowded city of Miami. There are unspoiled beaches and self-guided nature trails. The beaches here were the first ones to which black people had access in Miami. But developers would love to build luxury condominiums here, and the city stands to make a lot of money if it sells the land. A volunteer guide at the old lighthouse on Key Biscayne told us that a compromise was in the works. If history is any guide, rich folks will soon have another place to live. Once capital gets its foot in the door, it does not tolerate compromises. A few miles away at Miami Beach, a large and beautiful public beach is routinely used as private property by the wealthy. In late November 2004, jewelry magnate David Yurman and his wife Sybil had a warehouse-size tent, designed to look like a chic lounge, constructed on the beach, complete with several industrial air conditioners, to house a lavish dinner party in honor of the charitable work of the Cuban-born "*gusano*" singer Gloria Estefan and her husband Emilio. A few yards away, homeless people tried to get some sleep.

I have reached one major conclusion from what I have witnessed. The radical politics of the future must make inequality and environmental destruction its centerpieces. Both phenomena are so much a part of the nature of capitalism that it is hard to talk about them without making at least a partial indictment of the system. Their consequences are thoroughly harmful to the health, welfare, and happiness of the majority of people. They lend an ugliness to daily life that is becoming increasingly hard to tolerate. This is why some people turn to the seeming verities of religion. But I know from long experience as a teacher, mainly of working men and women, that discussion and analysis of these twin evils resonate strongly. We just have to find the ways and the means to hammer the effects of these evils home, over and over, in our unions, at our workplaces, in our political work, in letters to the editor, in our daily conversations.

Notes

1   The data on income and wealth distribution and on racial and ethnic income and wealth differences are taken from Lawrence Mishel, Jared Bernstein, and Sylvia Allegretto, The State of Working America, 2004–05 (Ithaca, N.Y.: Cornell University Press, 2005).
2   Edward Abbey, The Journey Home: Some Words in Defense of the American West (New York: E. P. Dutton, 1977), 187.
3   Edward Abbey, One Life at a Time, Please (New York: Henry Holt and Company, 1978), 60.

4   http://lightparty.com/Economic/Environmyou wrotentalFacts.html. This pollution continues today. In 2015, "The American Lung Association's 'State of the Air 2015' report found that 138.5 million people, or 44 percent of the U.S. population, live in counties where ozone or particle pollution makes the air unhealthy to breathe." See http://cbsnews.com/news/american-lung-association-air-quality-report-2015/

5   Greg Schneider, "Slowdown Forces Many to Wander for Work," Washington Post, November 9, 2004.

6   David Brooks, On Paradise Drive (New York: Simon & Schuster, 2004).

7   Forrest Norman, "Screwed If by Sea: Cruise Lines Throw Workers Overboard When It Comes to Providing Urgent Medical Care," Miami New Times, http://miamine wtimes.com/issues/2004-11-11/news/feature.html

8   For some good material on the national parks, including that which is mentioned in this article, see Philip Burnham, Indian Country, God's Country: Native Americans and the National Parks (Washington, D.C.: Island Press, 2000).

9
CESAR

Labor unions have always been equalizers. That is, they reduce inequality in several ways. First, they diminish the gap between the two great classes of our society, that between capital and labor. Some of the gains in wages, benefits, and working conditions they force upon employers reduces surplus labor time and hence profits. The rich get a little less rich, and the poor get a bit less poor. Labor unions also agitate for political reforms that benefit all workers, again, at least to some extent, at the expense of capital. Labor laws, health and safety legislation, and income maintenance programs empower workers by reducing their dependence on employers and easing the fear and insecurity that are an integral part of working-class life. By moderating inequality, unions also lessen the harm inequality does to mental and physical health. Second, unions reduce the income divide within the working class. They do this by winning collective bargaining agreements that set a wage for any given job, no matter who performs it. Irrespective of race, ethnicity, education, or age, if you do a job, you will be paid the same as anyone else who does it. Unions also compress the distribution of wages by negotiating the largest percentage wage increases for the lowest paid workers. Success here encourages low wage workers to seek unionization, and this further narrows wage differentials.[1]

Yet, while unions have been a powerful force for equality, they have lost much of their strength over the past forty years, victim of relentless employer and state antagonism and repression. They have also all too often succumbed to the blandishments of capitalism. U.S. union officers are the highest paid in the world, and there are more of them relative to membership than anywhere else. They are as a whole the most corrupt as well. They are overly bureaucratic and inclined to cut deals with employers that disempower the rank-and-file.[2]

At their best, unions and the labor movement have stirred heroic and unselfish actions by millions of people. One of the last inspirational unions was the United Farm Workers (UFW), which under the leadership of the charismatic Cesar Chavez built a union among the poorest and most exploited workers in the country. The UFW generated a nationwide movement of supporters and an army of mostly young volunteers who built a feared boycott machinery and did all of the small and large chores that made the union successful beyond anyone's dreams. At one point in the 1970s, some members were surely the most highly paid farm laborers in the world. Lettuce harvesters earned a wage the equivalent of over $50 per hour in today's prices.[3]

Unfortunately the UFW crashed and burned, in part because of employer violence and government hostility, but in part because of internal failures. When the union began to fade in the 1980s, an opportunity was lost to organize a majority of California's farm workers and their brothers and sisters in other states, and more importantly, to spearhead the building of a more radical and militant labor movement, one that might have been able to resist the neoliberal onslaught that marked the tremendous increase in inequality we have witnessed for so long.

I drove into union headquarters at 1:15 in the morning. It was raining, and I barely saw the sign for Keene, California, which was where my directions said to turn right from Route 66. Two hours before, I had eaten at a truck stop in Needles and begun driving across the desert. Now I was in the mountains, west of Tehachapi, heading toward Bakersfield. Keene wasn't on the California map in my road atlas, so I wasn't expecting much of a town. In fact, there was no town at all, just the Keene Café, Ed and Edna Melton, proprietors. It was closed so I couldn't stop to ask directions. I kept driving up the narrow road and about a mile later, I saw a hand-painted sign on a small post which read "La Paz: United Farm Workers of America." I turned my head back to the road just in time to brake before I ran over the guard who was flagging me to stop. The guard motioned me into a driveway blocked by a gate. A second guard approached my car from a small guardhouse, shined a light in my face, and asked me in a strongly accented voice what was my business. It didn't sound like they were expecting me. I found out later that the scheduled guards had been told, but they had traded shifts with two compañeros and forgotten to tell them. Ordinarily this wouldn't have mattered, but death threats had been made against union president Chavez and the guards were cautious of strangers. I told the second guard my name, that I had come to work for the union, and that I was expected. I gave him the name of my contact, Bill Martin, the union's personnel director. He had a conversation in Spanish with the other guard, who went into the booth and made a telephone call. Then he came out and, in a friendly tone said, "Welcome to the Farm Workers."

Within minutes, Bill Martin appeared on foot, introduced himself, said something to the guards and got into my car. "I'll show you your room. You must be tired. You can get some sleep and we'll talk tomorrow. I'll stop by for you at 7:00." I looked at my watch—2:00. I would still be tired in the morning. I had left Johnstown, Pennsylvania on New Year's Day, 1977, with an abscessed tooth, and by the time I reached Amarillo, Texas, I was taking fifteen aspirins a day without much effect. Suddenly, a pain shot through my jaw so sharp that I had to stifle a cry. I had a feeling that my next good night's sleep would be awhile in coming.

As he opened the door, Bill Martin was saying something about how they hadn't had time to clean my room. I was thinking, well, how bad could it be, until I looked inside. I'm glad he didn't look at me just then because my face must have reflected my immediate impulse to turn around and run. The room was filthy, an inch of dust on the floor, trash covering nearly every surface, furnished only with an ancient iron bed, a dirty sagging chair, and a scarred cupboard tilting dangerously forward. I wondered if maybe this was a test given to new recruits to measure their commitment right from the start. But Bill was talking cheerfully about how this was one of the nicer rooms, just a bit messy. I could get it shipshape in no time. I tried to duplicate Bill's cheerfulness. "It looks fine. Anyway, I'm so tired, I could sleep anywhere tonight. See you at seven." I lied about sleeping. No way was I going to rest now. I spent the next two hours cleaning the room as best I could, manically sweeping, shaking, and wiping. By 4:00 a.m. the room was presentable, at least in the dim light cast by the bare bulb hanging from the ceiling. I walked down the hall to the shower, but it didn't work. I washed myself with cold water, went back to my room and fell asleep. I dreamt that I was the preacher in *The Grapes of Wrath* addressing a large crowd of farm workers. I was talking about the loaves and fishes. Here in these rich valleys there were loaves and fishes aplenty, yet we who grew them went hungry. The rich men's tables were filled to overflowing yet ours were bare. Where was the justice in that? The growers were like vampires sucking our blood, and it sure couldn't be the will of Jesus, that poor savior of us all, that we just sit here and take it. The faces in the crowd nodded approval. I could feel their power. One of them shouted out, "Hey preacher, don't forget, we want clean rooms too."

"You probably won't be able to start working right away. Each new staff person has to meet with Cesar first, and he won't be back until next week." This was disappointing news. Bill had indeed knocked on my door at 7:00. He had taken me to his "kitchen" for coffee, introduced me to some of his friends, and escorted me on a tour of the grounds. The union's headquarters were located in what had been a private sanitarium for alcoholics. The owner, the son of an actor of some notoriety, had donated it to the union, making him about as popular as anthrax among the local cattle and horse ranchers. It was an isolated place, tucked into the desert mountains along the railroad tracks, about two miles from the famous horseshoe curve. The sanitarium had consisted of a large hospital and several outbuildings. Single staff persons lived in the hospital, while married staff lived in small houses or trailers.

Living arrangements were varied and informal. At one time, evening meals had been taken communally in a large refectory, but chronic labor shortages had made it impossible to continue this practice. Now staff persons were responsible for their own provisioning and cooking. In the hospital, people had more or less spontaneously formed "kitchens" of six to twelve members who constituted a sort of mini-collective for shopping and cooking. Bill invited me to join his kitchen, an offer I quickly accepted. He explained that my duties would include preparing supper for 8 to 10 people two or three times a month and collecting money and shopping for food maybe once a month. Over coffee I surveyed the kitchen. There was a double hotplate, an electric frying pan, a coffee pot, a few pots, pans, and plates, a motley and small collection of utensils, a beat up table, six broken chairs, a small bathroom sink and an ancient refrigerator. No stove, no real sink, and, I was casually informed, no hot water, which didn't matter because the water was contaminated and had to be boiled anyway. My stomach churned in panic. I couldn't cook for eight people in Julia Child's kitchen let alone here. When a woman sitting with us pointed to the cooking sign-up sheet on the refrigerator and suggested that I might as well sign it now, I looked at her with glazed eyes. There was a hint of sarcasm in her voice. She knew I was in trouble and was enjoying it. In fact, she had frowned when Bill had invited me to join their group. Mechanically, I surveyed the sheet and, with relief, I saw that there were open days at the end of the month. I marked them and made a mental note to write to my mother for recipes.

I wondered aloud what I was supposed to do until I could meet with Cesar. Bill suggested that I introduce myself to as many people as possible and let them know that I was available for work. He had heard that I would be working in the research office. Cesar had seemed excited when Bill had shown him my application. Bill had read it and decided that my skills might be better used here at union headquarters than in the Detroit office which was where I had originally been assigned. Cesar agreed, and this pleased Bill greatly. Cesar had said that, hey, we can get professors on our side too.

A lot of the people I met that first week were new, and there were frequent references to people who had just left. This didn't surprise me—

low wages, hard work, and substandard living conditions have a way of wearing down people's commitment. The new people were uniformly idealistic and happy to be here. Most were in their early twenties and had supported the union in college or in their churches. To all of us the union was special, an uncorrupted champion of the poorest workers, and Cesar was a hero, a mystical little man, a modern-day Gandhi, who, through sheer determination and will, had finally beaten the growers. He had built a union and a movement. The campesinos flocked to his union, and people who wanted to do something right with their lives flocked to his movement. With monastic zeal we came to the union, to do good and I suppose, to purify our souls.

On first meeting, union veterans seemed just as idealistic and selfless as the newcomers. Within a few days I felt more at home than I imagined possible. This was a true community, and I found myself thinking that I should quit teaching and move here. I felt separated from my former self, as if I were in the middle of a spiritual reawakening. One evening a married couple took me to a local union meeting in a small town down the mountain. About two hundred workers talked and sang in Spanish and English, loyalists, none of whom had yet won union contracts but who had marched and picketed from San Francisco to Boston, giving witness for the union. "Yo soy economista," I repeated again and again. They smiled a silent welcome or told me their stories in broken English. I was moved, happy to be with brothers and sisters.

"You can go in now." I had been waiting in Cesar's outer office for an hour, ignored by his personal secretary, a young Anglo named Mark Wilson. Mark was flanked by two assistants, another Anglo and a handsome Chicano, Juan Salazar, who was Cesar's chief bodyguard. They were not a friendly group. They made me uncomfortable, especially Mark, who reminded me of a type of person who feels that he has the absolute right to order people around because he is close to the person who can. When Juan looked at me, I remembered that I had seen him the night before arguing with a woman I assumed to be his wife. Their child was crying and his wife was saying loudly that he should spend more time with his son. Juan spoke sharply to her—when he saw me, he glared but then smiled and said "Buenos noches, hermano." Today

I remembered the glare. My meeting lasted less than five minutes. Mark followed me into a spare, windowless office and introduced me to Cesar. He was a small, slightly built man with jet black hair, dressed in a cheap open-collared shirt, chino pants, and sandals. He shook my hand limply but with both hands. He had a gentle voice and manner. He spoke directly and without pause, explaining what he had in mind for me to do. He wanted me to attend a staff conference in Stockton the following weekend. Then the meeting was over. At the door I turned to ask a question. Cesar looked up at me from his desk. I was too embarrassed to speak so I smiled and left.

Stockton is about 40 miles east of San Francisco, a shabby town, squat and dirty, like most of those in California's central valleys. In summer the temperature reaches 110 degrees, and the air is fouled by pesticides. We had arrived in Stockton late at night after a long drive: Cesar, two bodyguards, and me. We stayed at the house of a union supporter. Cesar knew thousands of people and, like an Indian holy man, never had to worry about a place to eat and to sleep. It was my 31st birthday, and I had packed a bottle of wine. We drank it after the meal and a meeting with a union lawyer. Cesar toasted me. He said that I was doing good work for the union.

My job in Stockton was to testify in an unfair labor practice hearing. Under pressure from the union, its allies, and a sympathetic governor, California's legislature had enacted a law which gave farm workers the right to organize unions and negotiate contracts without employer interference. Most growers had reacted to the law with contempt and continued to treat their workers like peons and unions as the work of communist agitators. Once the union had organized a ranch, it had to get the employer to the bargaining table. More often than not the growers refused to go.

Stockton was a hotbed of grower defiance of the law, complete with terrorist vigilante groups. The alleged leader of the vigilantes was one Ernest Carvalho Jr., a tomato grower and labor contractor. Mr. Carvalho had a fearsome reputation, having once yanked a union organizer up from the ground by his mustache. He had once met the server of a labor board subpoena with a shotgun. During the organizing campaign, two of his workers, union supporters, had been savagely beaten. No one doubted that the attacker had been paid by Carvalho. Miraculously the union had won the election, but Carvalho had refused to recognize and bargain with it, forcing the union to file charges. My job was to testify as to how much money Carvalho's refusal to bargain had cost the campesinos. Cesar would testify too, because this was the first case of its kind. A large judgment against the grower would send a strong message to others.

We arrived at the municipal building early. Our lawyers had to talk to some of the witnesses, farm workers huddled in a group at the rear of the room. They were tense and fearful, but the sight of Cesar eased them greatly. He had a bond with them difficult to describe but readily seen. He was of them but above them. He was their leader; he had asked them to be here; they were here. As he spoke with them, I thought of the Zapatistas in Orozco's painting. Like them, these campesinos stood straight and tall in front of their commander, in sharp contrast to their stooped and suppliant bodies out in the fields.

By the start of the hearing, the small room was packed. The rows of folding chairs were separated by a narrow center aisle. We sat on the left, Carvalho and company on the right. I read a book once which said that *The Grapes of Wrath* was not a great novel because the growers were presented as one-dimensionally evil people. This critic should have seen this crew. Big bellied, fat-jowled, cold-eyed men dressed in jeans and boots and cowboy hats, sniggering among themselves, giving us hard stares. They looked exactly like pigs, and Carvalho was their pig-leader. When I glanced at him, I had an image of his strangling Cesar with his bare hands, grunting, spit dripping from his chin. I was sure that he stank no matter how many showers he took. No, these were evil people. They were capable of unprovoked violence. Had I thought about it, I would have argued that Steinbeck had been too generous. Because up and down the valleys there are men like these. They are the bedrock of California agriculture, the shock troops for the big corporate growers with their smooth-as-silk lawyers and suave manners, who wouldn't think of beating or hitting a farm worker but wouldn't mourn her death either.

The hearing was raucous and unruly. We petitioned to have testimony translated into Spanish, but the judge refused. He said we would never finish a bilingual hearing, but then he had to admonish us to keep quiet a dozen times as we whispered translations to the campesinos. Carvalho stood up and shouted that he "wasn't gonna negotiate with no bunch of goddam comanists." He said, "I'm just a dumb fuckin' Portagee, but I ain't dealin' with no comanists." When the judge warned him about his language, he grinned and said, "I don't know no other words. I'm just a dumb Portagee." His lawyer tried to calm him, but Carvalho shoved him away. He pointed at Cesar and taunted, "Hey Cesar. Let's me and you settle this. Let's go in the next room. Me and you. If you come out first, I'll recognize your commie union. If I come out, hey, we'll just all go home and forget this fuckin' hearing." Cesar sat immobile and stared ahead, but his bodyguards tensed. The judge kept pounding his gavel, but his power had deserted him. I turned to watch the other growers. The only thin man among them returned my stare with a grin. He made his hand into a gun and silently pulled the trigger. Carvalho said, "See, you're not a man, just a fuckin' comanist." The judge recessed the hearing until the next morning. When the union asked for Carvalho's employment records, which had been subpoenaed and which he had brought with him in a large cardboard box, Carvalho snapped them up and strode out of the room.

Cesar was not a good speaker. His voice was soft, and he possessed none of the tricks of the speaker's trade: the pregnant pause, the change of rhythm, the crescendo, the pointing finger. He was utterly without physical powers. Yet right away, he captivated you, made you listen, made you want to do what he said. He had a way of making you feel like an important person, that what you were telling him could change the course of the union, put it over the top of that long hill it had been climbing so slowly. Maybe it was his eyes. They were guileless eyes, the eyes of a child. You could not refuse them.

He was a master of symbolic action. He often played the saint, fasting like Gandhi, adding power by subtracting it. He would carry a cross on Good Friday, staggering under its weight, suffering for those whose lives are bounded by the short-handled hoe, the endless march, the early death. Once he had to appear in court to answer charges that union members had ambushed a train and shot rifle bullets into refrigerator cars. The local papers were full of righteous editorials and grower letters which accused the union of shameful hypocrisy, preaching but not practicing nonviolence. On the day of the hearing, some 2000 members and supporters lined the street leading up to the county courthouse and the steps and hallways leading to the courtroom. Cesar walked between them, staggering from a recent fast. The crowd remained eerily silent; only Cesar and the police moved. When he reached the topmost step, everyone knelt down, in unison, with machine-like precision. Within an hour, all of the charges had been dropped.

Every Saturday afternoon, we went out to the fields surrounding our compound to work in the garden. Sometimes this would be preceded by a community meeting in the morning. Presumably these were town meetings in which we would air our grievances and collectively govern ourselves. But while we would act like brothers and sisters, we were clearly the children of Cesar. He ran the meetings, and we discussed what he wanted to discuss. Flanked by his farting and belching guard dogs, Cesar would command us, cajole us, mock us, threaten us, all the while pretending that everyone was equal. I loved these meetings at first, but I soon noticed that it was dangerous to criticize Cesar. Once he told us that a friend of the union wanted to donate several washing machines and dryers, but he wasn't sure he would accept them because we wouldn't take care of them. We'd fucked up everything else. We couldn't keep the place clean. There was dog shit all over the place. Around the room hands shot up. Did Cesar realize that we had to drive fifteen miles to do laundry which meant we had to have access to a car. And laundry costs money which nobody had. One person's complaint gave the next person courage, and soon the room was a babble of complaining voices. Cesar was unimpressed. He simply said that he really didn't care about this chickenshit. He didn't have to worry about his laundry anyway. This macho response was met by a chorus of boos. Cesar's eyes narrowed and his mouth tightened. He spat out, "I work eighteen fucking hours a day, every day. For the union. Which of you can say the same? You're wasting my time with this chickenshit."

We sat very still for more than a minute. Ricardo Reyes, the union's treasurer, said, "Cesar, don't forget about the water." Cesar's voice softened and he told us that we could once again drink the water. With that the meeting ended.

I liked the gardening, at least in small doses. It was good to use my muscles after sitting at a desk all week. And working on a community project with a true melting pot of humanity—Filipinos, Mexicans, Anglos, men and women, young and old—gave me a feeling that the muck and slime of the real world could be overcome and as the song went, "peace would rule the planet and love would steer the stars." Cesar loved the garden. He was an expert on organic gardening and lectured us about its subtleties from the proper fertilizer to planting by the moon. After a while we would break for a picnic lunch, and he would tell us something of the history of the union. We were eager disciples. He spun his stories of the growers and the campesinos as Christ must have told his parables. People lowered their heads to hide their tears.

Then we had to return to work, monotonous and physically exhausting in the 80 degree February heat and high altitude. Guilt kept me hard at it, long after the warm glow of brotherhood had worn off. I wanted nothing more than to go back to my room, shower, change clothes and begin my "day off." I would race down the mountain to Bakersfield, which after a week of isolation at La Paz, had been transformed in my mind, from the nation's biggest truck stop, carrot capital of the world, and birthplace of Merle Haggard, into a shining metropolis. I would rent a room in the Downtowner Motel, order cartons of Chinese food, eat myself sick, take a long bath, and sleep until noon. Or I'd take some friends and go to a Mexican bar to shoot pool and drink beer. We could go to a place where we would be the only Anglos and not worry about a racial confrontation because we were with the union, though it wasn't wise to root against the Mexican boxer who would be fighting on the television above the bar. Only a few more wheelbarrows of manure. Only a few more blisters on my hand. I was glad I had a little money and happy I wasn't a farm worker.

As best I can tell, the trouble began with the mail announcement. I had been in Oxnard helping a local negotiate a piece rate proposal with a tomato grower. The grower, William Fontin, prided himself as an intellectual, a libertarian who loved Barry Goldwater and William F. Buckley. More than a few economists are libertarians. They babble about free markets and free choice and individual liberty, but when their privileges are threatened, as when the lower orders have the nerve to form, say, a union, they are quick to put on their jackboots and goose step. Fontin was no exception, although I was amused by the slogan he had printed on every box of his tomatoes, "Unsubsidized Product of the Free Capitalist Economy of the United States." He smoked a pipe and was usually polite, but he would agree to nothing. He refused to negotiate in Spanish though he spoke it fluently. He referred to me as "that professor of yours." I had gotten to know the union negotiating team. The handsome president of the committee had invited me to a party at his house where I'd gotten drunk enough on tequila to dance. I wanted to help, but we were just going through the motions. Fontin was as tough as Carvalho. He wouldn't settle until the workers showed that they could make his tomatoes rot on the vine.

When I returned to La Paz, I heard about the mail fiasco from two of my friends, Daniel and Carl. They came to my room, looking up and down the hall before closing the door. "Did you hear about the mail shit?" said Daniel. "Orders from Cesar. From now on all of your mail is going to be opened before you get it." "You're kidding," I said, wondering to myself if anything in any letters to me could be suspect. "Why?" "They say it's because some contributions people sent to the union are missing, but that's bull shit. It's just more of Cesar's paranoia."

I think that I had been waiting for something bad to happen. Right before I had gone off to do the piece rate proposal, Cesar had asked for volunteers to participate in some kind of retreat at a drug and alcohol rehabilitation place run by a friend of his. This place had achieved some notoriety complete with an exposé in the local newspapers. It seems that the founder, Ron Wood, had become something of a guru and his organization a spiritual center with its own unique methods for curing drug addiction. Each newly admitted addict was compelled to participate in the "game" as Ron called it. The game was nothing more than a thought control device, common to many cults. People in the group would gang up on the new people, accusing them of all sorts of bad deeds while at the same time giving them maximum attention. Combined with sleep deprivation and a bad diet, this regimen often succeeds in making people feel helpless unless they give themselves up to the group. Given a benign reading, this may be just what a person, whose being has been destroyed by drugs, needs, a new life so to speak. A more cynical person might see in this a form of mind control aimed primarily at enhancing the power of the leader. My instinct told me that the latter interpretation was more likely to be true. My gut reaction was reinforced when someone told me that Ron's disciples had placed a poisonous snake in the mailbox of the reporter who had written the exposé. Ominously, the people chosen to be in the game were all in Cesar's inner circle of relatives, bodyguards, and personal aides.

Gossip about the mail and the game abounded. A young maintenance worker, Roger, boldly posted a petition protesting the opening of our mail. I signed it, and so did most of my friends. This created a lot of tension. People began to avoid us, and most people stopped talking about anything which had to do with the union. I began to suspect that Cesar's bodyguards were watching us carefully. One of them mysteriously showed up at the first session of a labor history class which some staff had asked me to teach. No one with whom I was close volunteered for the game.

The tension was broken somewhat by two events—Cesar's 50th birthday party and the trip to Los Angeles to campaign for the mayor. Hundreds of notables came to the party. We started it out at 6:00 in the morning with a serenade at Cesar's house complete with mariachi band and many shots of tequila. Then we ate menudo (tripe soup) to ward off the effects of the liquor and took up our posts at the giant barbecue in honor of our leader. My job was to dole out the sauce, a fiery concoction which went on the meat and rice. The Anglos would say "not too much," but the Mexicans would say "más, más." During a break, I went to my office to get a book, and I came upon a famous actress, brave critic of the war in Vietnam, bitching at her kids for tormenting Cesar's dogs. "Can't you children behave anywhere?" she moaned. Even the rich and famous have their troubles, I thought.

I stumbled into bed hours later and fell right to sleep. But I was awakened too soon by the sounds of loud talking from the room across the hall. I put my ear up to my door and listened. I recognized the voices of two of Cesar's bodyguards. They were giving the third degree to Chris, one of the union's youngest volunteers. "Why did you sign the mail petition? You called Cesar a dictator! Man, you're a fucking traitor. Cesar wants you out of here. Tomorrow." When they left, I quietly went back to bed, too afraid to go over and comfort Chris.

The next week Cesar pulled the entire staff out of headquarters and into an abandoned high school in East Los Angeles. From here we were sent into the streets with farm workers from throughout the state to march door-to-door urging people to vote for the incumbent mayor. As usual Cesar gave us no warning, just orders. Some of the older staff were upset by this. The union had more pressing business, namely scores of organizing drives and numerous contracts to negotiate. They wondered aloud why we were doing this instead, especially since the mayor had little competition and eventually won by a large margin. I too thought that the trip was unnecessary, but the whole thing demonstrated again Cesar's amazing ability to get people to do what he wanted and the union's capacity to organize complex logistics on very short notice. East LA was pretty fascinating, like being in another country. The tiny houses and shabby apartments and hotels exuded poverty, but the pastel colors and warm breezes could deceive you. Somehow tropical poverty didn't seem as real from the outside as did the slums of the great Eastern cities. As I chatted in my bad Spanish with the campesina with whom I had been paired, I wondered what would happen when we got back to La Paz.

Cesar marched into the community meeting room followed by four of his bodyguards. Usually he would chat with someone seated in front and wait for us to stop talking so that the meeting could begin. But this time he just stood and stared at us as did the guards. From the rear came voices urging "quiet" and "shh." I quickly looked around the room. It was jammed; people were standing in the doorway on tiptoes craning to see. The sudden quiet was eerie because it was so unusual. Even the babies and young children were silent. The last sound I heard was a guitar chord. We always sang songs at our meetings, "No Nos Moverán" or "De Colores," but there would be no singing tonight.

"Some people here are trying to undermine the union." Cesar said this without emotion but he might just as well have screamed at us. I felt a knot forming in my stomach, and my throat became dry. I noticed that the bodyguards were still standing; two were wearing dark glasses, reminding me of Tonton Macoutes. Something was terribly wrong. "There's a cancer growing in the union. We know now that some people have gone over to the growers. We go to a fucking meeting and they knew our proposals. We plan to organize a ranch and they know about it before we fucking start. Some people here are traitors. And they're going to have to leave."

"Who are these bastards, Cesar?" said the chubby old man sitting next to me. He was a Filipino, Ricardo Ochoco, an officer of the union who had defended Cesar's tirade about the washing machines. There was a certain tension between Filipinos and Hispanics rooted in the fact that while the Filipino minority had actually started the union, the Hispanic majority, led by Cesar, had taken control of it, some said in a less than democratic manner. Cesar always spoke highly of the Filipino brothers and sisters, and Ochoco was proof of the multiethnic leadership of the union. But Ochoco was a weak man, a sycophant always trying to prove his loyalty to Cesar.

"Wait a minute, Cesar, how do you know?"—Juan Reyes, a tough little Chicano and chief of the maintenance staff, jumped up to ask a question, but he was drowned out before he could finish by shouts which seemed to come from all around the room. "Juan is one of them." "He's always complaining. His name is first on the mail protest." "He called Cesar a dictator." To my right, Nico, Cesar's youngest son, had stood up and was yelling, "Listen, listen." He reminded me of a puppet, waving his hands. Nico had never impressed me. He was a whiny teenager with an unpleasant nasal voice and without much talent as best I could tell. Like most of Cesar's inner circle, his main talent was to do what his father wanted. Like them he was nothing without Cesar.

"Listen, I think Juan is selling out the union. Juan Salazar saw him in Bakersfield talking to some growers. He's one of the leaders of a clique here, always badmouthing the union. At every meeting he opposes Cesar. He's a fucking traitor." At this, Juan Reyes made a rush for Nico but was quickly surrounded by the guards. "That's a bunch of fucking lies," he shouted. I waited for others to defend Juan but none did. Those that weren't shouting insults at him sat rigidly on the uncomfortable seats. They were afraid, and I was too. "Let him go." Cesar commanded. He walked over to Juan Reyes and said quietly, "Brother, you're screwing the union. It would be better if you left." Juan looked at him in disbelief. He was close to tears. I waited for him to respond, but he didn't. He just walked out of the room.

Before anyone could react, Maria Quinoñes, was pointing a finger at David Young who was sitting right next to me. "David is always with Juan Reyes. He's a traitor too." David tensed and looked directly at her. He had contempt for Maria as did I. She was the daughter of the union's first vice president, Domenica Quinoñes, a legendary union organizer who had faced down more than one gun and had been arrested countless times. But Maria was not the equal of her mother. She was nosy and obnoxious, La Casa's telephone operator and notorious for listening in on our calls. She often slept with Charlie, the guard, who occupied the room above me, keeping me awake with their noisy quarrels and lovemaking. Outside the union she was just another unpleasant person. You could ignore her. But here she was important. She could ruin your life, and she had just begun to ruin David's.

"You're full of shit." David said, but his words were drowned out by accusations from every corner of the room. The same stock phrases that had been hurled at Juan Reyes were now directed at David. It struck me suddenly that this had all been planned. This was "the game." This was what they had learned at Dalanon. I was witnessing the transformation of the union into a cult. A sense of detachment came over me, and I watched the "show trial" unfolding before me as if I were watching a horror movie, afraid but curious to see what would happen.

David stood up and demanded, "Am I on trial here. What are the charges, Cesar?"

"Isn't it true that you said that campaigning for Mayor Bradley was a waste of time?" Cesar was agitated and speaking in an uncharacteristically loud voice.

"So what. So did lots of people."

"Haven't you been criticizing me, saying chickenshit stuff behind my back, saying it was my fault the union lost the Initiative?"

"That's bull shit. Who told you that, that fucking wimp over there." David pointed at Nico, who took his cue to launch into a tirade, accusing David of being an agent for the growers. Other voices joined the chorus. No one spoke in David's defense.

Before he could be stopped, David hopped over two rows of chairs and stood next to Cesar. No one made a move to subdue him.

"Am I being charged?" David said. He was standing straight, almost at attention, dwarfing the diminutive Cesar beside him. The guards made a move toward him, but Cesar waved them away. David's actions had surprised him, threatening to unravel this carefully choreographed meeting. It was up to the rest of us now. Many of us were David's friends. None of us believed that he was an agent of the grower or anything else but a brother dedicated to the union. But he could never stand up to Cesar alone. Would we defend him?

"The union constitution says that no one can be expelled from the union without a fair hearing. What are the charges against me? Who is making them? I have a right to defend myself. This whole thing here tonight is illegal."

"You don't have any fucking rights, brother. You're working for the growers. We know it. You're a cancer here, a disease. Admit it, man. Hey, let's put it to a vote, right here. Who thinks David should go?"

The same voices that had been yelling for blood all night cried out in unison, "Go. Go. Go." Some others joined the chorus. Mark Wilson, Carlos's secretary, began to clap his hands. Soon the chanting and clapping filled the room, the noise rising to a fearsome level. Sweat glistened on the blank faces of the believers; they were in the grip of a religious frenzy. They wanted blood, and they would have it.

Suddenly Cesar raised his hands and silenced the howling mob. "Who thinks David should stay?" No one raised a hand. The ferocity of the crowd cowed us completely. I thought, maybe he is guilty. I was grateful that it wasn't me. I looked at Sister Denise. She was looking at me with sad and frightened eyes. Then she raised her hand. Cesar's eyes blazed at her with a look of genuine hatred, but he quickly looked away.

"See, brother. The community wants you to leave. Leave now brother." Cesar then addressed us in his usual soft voice. "This meeting is over. Don't forget. We'll be going to the garden tomorrow after Mass." Cesar's words broke the unbearable tension, and with visible relief, people began to file out of the room. But David did not move; he simply sat down on the floor and said, "I'm not leaving until I hear the charges against me and until I have a hearing." Cesar ignored him and walked away, speaking in Spanish to the guards. A few people glanced down at David as they passed but not many. Within a few minutes the room was empty except for David, Sister Denise, and myself. Someone had turned out the lights, and the darkness compounded the silence. I heard dogs barking, and a radio sounded faintly in the cool night air.

"David, are you alright," Sister Denise asked softly.

"Yeah, but I think we're in deep shit."

"What do you think they'll do?" My stomach felt the way it did when I told my wife I was in love with another woman. What had begun in such high spirits was ending in horror. My mind wandered crazily, but with its immediate focus on myself. How would I get my lecture notes, which my friends at school had mailed to me so that I could teach the class in labor history? Would the guards be visiting me tonight? Was I in physical danger? How would I get out of here? I wanted to be back on Route 66 headed east across the great desert.

"I think they're going to have me arrested. I think Cesar told Juan Salazar to get the police here."

"Arrested for what? Peacefully protesting this crazy shit? That would be some irony."

"No, for trespassing. You forgot. I don't live here anymore. Cesar threw me out."

"But what about the union's constitution? What about what's fucking right?"

"Cesar couldn't care less. And neither will the cops. Don't you know. Cesar is the law here, and it was pretty apparent that most people don't have a problem with that. But you two ought to get out of here. You haven't been accused of anything."

"No way. I didn't have the nerve to speak out in the meeting. I'm gonna stay. They can arrest me too."

"They won't. Cesar won't want a professor and a nun in jail. I'm just a carpenter, less likely to cause embarrassment you know."

"Maybe I should go talk to Cesar now," said Sister. "Tell him how crazy this is. Maybe this wasn't his idea. Maybe he's calmed down by now. Maybe . . ."

"Sister, don't you see. This whole thing was planned, by Cesar with his little group of flunkies. This was 'the game.' Juan Reyes and I were just its first victims."

We sat in the dark rooms and talked. La Paz seemed like a tomb, still as a stalking cat in the mountain desert. The only sounds we heard were those of the guards who were piling David's belongings on the walkway in front of his room. At least that's what we thought was happening after we heard a voice commanding, "Take his shit out to the sidewalk."

When the screen door slammed and heavy footsteps sounded on the hallway floor, I knew that David was right. Someone hit the light switch, and by the time my eyes focused, four cops were moving toward David. I made out the words "Mojave Police" on one of their badges.

The largest of the four, a red-faced man with a donut shop belly and a fat ass, said, "You David Young?" He seemed uneasy, as if he grasped the incongruity of arresting a union staff person at union headquarters. He'd busted a few union heads on picket lines and

stuck his billy club between the ribs of his share of Mexicans. That's
what cops did. But this was something different, new terrain, so
to speak, and he didn't have a map.

"That's me. What can I do for ya?"

"Just get up so I can get these cuffs on you. You're under
arrest."

"You gonna read me my rights?" The cop tensed and his face
turned crimson. One of the others tightened the grip on his billy
club and fingered his revolver.

"Don't get smart buddy. It was your folks called us out here. We
ain't never been here before. You must be a real bad actor. Now
just get up."

David didn't move and just looked up at the cop with an almost
whimsical expression on his face.

"I think he's on a sit-down strike. Ain't that right buddy?", said
one of the fat cop's partners. "We're gonna hafta carry him out.
Good thing there's four of us. He's a big fella."

"Suit yourself. By the way, what are the charges?"

"They say you're trespassing. They asked you to leave and you
said 'fuck you'"

"That's a lie, he never said that," I shouted. "And how can he
be trespassing? He lives here. I'll show you his room."

"That's not what they say. You got proof you live here. A lease
or something."

"What do you think?" David said. "Look, just carry me out of
here and get it over with. That's what you're here for. You got TV
at your jail?"

"You're such a wise ass, buddy, maybe we'll just . . ."

"Shut up, Joe," spit the big cop, glaring over at us. "Yeah, big
guy, we got all the amenities of home. You'll see." He looked at
his men and said, "Grab him." Then they carried him out. We
followed them to the police car and watched as they shoved him
in the middle of the back seat and drove away.

"Sister, I'm getting the hell out of here, now. I'm packing my
stuff and I'll drive up to Mojave and try to bail David out of jail.

What about you?" "I have to stay. I'll try to put David's things in my room."

I don't have a very clear memory of the next few days. I did bail David out of jail. One of our friends, Leila, the union organizer who was negotiating with Mr. Fontin in Oxnard, called her parents in San Jose and made arrangements for David to stay with them for a while. I drove him there and stayed the night. Leila's parents were old left Communists, appalled that their daughter had converted to Catholicism, the better to serve the campesinos. The next morning I headed south and then east toward home.

The Grapes of Wrath was published in 1939. A lot has changed since then; a lot of working people began to make a fairly good living, even buy good cars and houses and send their kids to school. But for farm workers the changes haven't been so great. They're still dirt poor. They're still sickly, from lousy food, from pesticides, from fouled water. They still don't often live past 50. And their kids still don't go to school. Their skin colors change, but their lives don't. And what's true here is true everywhere in the world where the big growers own the land. Money is what they want, money in a ceaseless and growing flow, and the way to get it is to have a large reserve army of people without land whose only choice is to harvest the crops for nothing or die. The big growers will do whatever they have to do, including kill people outright, to insure the existence of the landless masses. And this is true in the U.S.A., in Mexico, in El Salvador, in the Philippines, in Indonesia, everywhere the land and its bounty have become merely things to buy and sell.

But everywhere the big growers enslave people, some of the people catch on. Some of them figure it out themselves, and some of them get help from the few outsiders who care. They come to understand why they are poor while the bosses are rich. It's a simple thing really but hard to learn, because the whole of the power of all of the forces that run a society—the owners, the presses, the schools, the churches, the government—have been blanketing the people with a heavy weight of lies. Of course, it's a dangerous thing too; in most parts of the world, you'll risk your life to learn it. Yet still some do learn the great truth, that profits and poverty, profits and landlessness go together. Just like winter and snow in the mountains, where there is one, there is the other. And these people, when they learn the truth, have to act on it. They have to tell others, and then they and the others and the outsiders are transformed. They begin to form study groups, base communities, coops, credit unions, labor unions. They meet, they march, they strike, they form armies and they fight—to get the land back, to make a decent wage, to live a life of dignity. The big people don't like this, and they torture and kill and bribe and lie to stop it. Most times it stops, but sometimes the poor people win and when they do, they leave a lesson for those who follow, those who must finally make the land and all of the earth's wealth the equal property of all.

Cesar was one of the people who caught on and then did something about it. What he did was wonderful, magnificent really. He built a union where none had ever been able to exist. He gave people a vision, and the vision made them do things they'd never been able to do before. Mute people gained voices and spread the word across the land. We are poor, but we know why, we know what to do, and we're going to do it. Up and down the valley, they formed their unions and won their contracts, and the growers took heed and were afraid.

But any movement of the poor is a fragile thing; it will be beset by demons from without and within. The external enemies are well-known, constant irritants and often overwhelmingly powerful. Those inside the union are more subtle yet nearly as destructive: leaders have big and conflicting egos; sexual and racial tensions are hard to overcome; people have honest differences about goals and strategies; it is enormously difficult to create the selfless bureaucracy which alone will insure the movement's continuity. Cesar learned how to get power and to use it effectively to combat the union's external foes, but such power was also used inside to solidify his personal hold on the movement. As he did this, he came to see the movement as his movement, to shape as he pleased. Anyone inside opposed to him was quickly branded as an outside enemy and excised from the union. His movement was not strong enough to contain him, and the results were like those I have described above.

In the years since then, things have gotten much worse. Nearly every officer, organizer, and lawyer was been purged or quit. Most of the membership drifted away, because the union could not keep them under contract with the growers and would not tolerate rank-and-file criticism of Cesar. The current president of the union, Arturo Rodriquez, is Cesar's son-in-law, a man who talks as if the union is still relevant to the lives of farm workers but has not done much to make it so. I wrote in a review of Miriam Pawel's fine book, *The Union of Their Dreams*:

He [Rodriquez] does appear to have a talent for overseeing, along with Cesar's son Paul and other family members and assorted scoundrels, an empire—begun by Chavez himself—of housing developments, radio stations, consulting enterprises, mass-mailing fund-raising campaigns, and marketing schemes (UFW paraphernalia, Chavez mementos, and the like). Meanwhile, pensions and health funds are awash in cash, but precious few workers get any benefits. In a labor movement notorious for corruption and shortchanging the membership, the United Farm Workers has secured a place on the union wall of infamy.[4]

In 1995, Cesar died at the age of 66. He was a great man, but, for the campesinos' sake, I hope that no one arises to take his place. In the end, a proletarian dictator is no better than any other.

Notes

1   Lawrence Mishel, et al. The State of Working America, 12th Edition (Ithaca, N.Y.: ILR Press, 2012), chapter 4 ("Wages").
2   Michael D. Yates, Why Unions Matter, 2nd Edition (New York: Monthly Review Press, 2009); Michael D. Yates, "Trumka and Hoffa Babble While the House of Labor Burns," http://cheapmotelsandahotplate.org/2011/09/17/hoffa-and-trumka-babble-while-the-house-of-labor-burns/
3   Frank Bardacke, Trampling Out the Vintage: Cesar Chavez and the Two Souls of the United Farm Workers (New York: Verso, 2011).
4   Michael D. Yates, "The Rise and Fall of the United Farm Workers," Monthly Review, 62/1, (May 2010); Miriam Pawel, The Union of Their Dreams: Power, Hope, and Struggle in Cesar Chavez's Farm Worker Movement (New York: Bloomsbury Press, 2009).

10
OWS AND THE IMPORTANCE OF POLITICAL SLOGANS

Slogans, rallying cries, and phrases that catch our attention are all necessary components of political campaigns, wars, and revolutions. In our age of social media, they are probably more essential than ever. They strike at our deepest emotions and elucidate what is at the heart of a struggle in a way that a long, detailed analysis cannot. The most important phrases in the continuing battle against inequality are "The 1 percent" and "We are the 99 percent." These have exploded across the world and continue to energize those whose futures have been increasingly darkened by the growing power of the rich.

Radical political movements always employ slogans that encapsulate in a few powerful words the aspirations of those fighting for a new world. The French revolutionaries fought under the banner, "Liberty, Equality, Fraternity," words that still resonate with radicals. The first words of the U.S. Constitution—"We the People"—have quickened the hearts of generations of populist activists. Emiliano Zapata's soldiers longed for "Tierra y Libertad," and the peasant armies of Mao Tse Tung went to war for "Land to the Tiller."

Every slogan has a context, circumstances that give rise to the words and make them effective. For example, when the Chinese communists were waging their long struggle against the army of Chiang Kai-shek, they relied upon mass support from peasants, who formed the base of the Red Army. China was still a largely feudal society, and peasants were brutally exploited by rich landlords. Those who worked the land wanted it, and the communists promised to give it to them. "Land to the Tillers" expressed this desire and the Party's commitment to it. Even today, after decades of capitalist restoration, China's rural people still have land rights won in revolutionary struggle.

The catchphrases of political upheaval are always somewhat vague. In China, there were the farmers who tilled the soil and the landlords who owned it. However, both classes included people of varying economic means. There were small, medium, and large landholders. Not all peasants lived in squalor and destitution. Yet, all landlords tended to be lumped together, and all of their land was fair game for expropriation.

The imprecise nature of political slogans is a virtue. Actual political programs do not derive from words alone but from the balance of class forces that exist at a particular point in time. What slogans do is clarify the most basic political cleavages; they help people develop the mindset most suited to active participation in whatever struggles are at hand. In China, "land to the tiller" said that those who worked the land should possess it; those who owned but did not till, should not. That some both owned and tilled did not and should not have mattered. Such complexities would have to be dealt with later, when a new constellation of class forces had come into being.

The worldwide Occupy movement that erupted in Manhattan's Zuccotti Park in September 2011 took as its watchwords, "We are the 99 percent." These words resonated with large masses of people as few others have in a long while. To understand why, it's important to look at the context that generated the slogan.

"We are the 99 percent" derived its power from the devastation experienced by so many people during the Great Recession that erupted in December of 2007. The roots of this economic crisis go back to the mid-1970s, when an employer-led attack upon the working class began in response to lower corporate profit margins, the result of the declining global economic dominance of the United States. U.S. businesses faced strong economic competitors in Japan and Europe; the costs of the War in Vietnam were generating inflation and higher wages; and the brisk demand for U.S. capital goods diminished as the rest of the world completed post-Second World War reconstruction.

A weakened and class-collaborationist labor movement accommodated a rapid victory by capital, in what we typically call neoliberalism: a political project that included the deregulation of finance, privatization of public services, elimination and curtailment of social welfare programs, open attacks on unions, and routine violations of labor laws. These left working people with lower wages, less generous benefits, and growing insecurity.

The deregulation of capital markets gave rise to a host of new financial instruments, which grew by leaps and bounds as cash-strapped workers began to go into debt by borrowing against their houses and maxing out their credit cards. All of this generated growing income and wealth inequality; raised the financial sector to the commanding heights of the economy; and made production more vulnerable to financial crisis. The Great Recession was the product of the interaction of these three factors, and it brought forth worldwide misery not seen since the 1930s. While the downturn officially ended in June 2009, much of the working class is still mired in debt, employed in low wage/no benefit jobs, either unemployed or fearful of job loss, and not very hopeful about the future.

While there were periodic protests against neoliberalism, it was not until the Great Recession that these broke out into mass struggle. This first emerged in the Arab Spring, but it soon spread to the entire world, from Spain to China and from Canada to Chile. In the United States, the Wisconsin Uprising of early 2011, led by public employees, inspired workers across the country, demonstrating that when pushed hard enough, in the right circumstances the working class would revolt and do things no one had imagined possible. Then, within a year of this, OWS erupted. Young people, led mainly by anarchists, took over Zuccotti Park in downtown Manhattan and waged protests against one of the greatest symbols of the 1 percent—Wall Street. When the police began to suppress the dissent, thousands of Occupy supporters descended upon the center of finance. Soon amazing displays of cooperative action and self-education deepened the struggle.

As the OWS phenomenon spread to cities and towns in the United States and then the world, the objects of the protestors' scorn and anger increased geometrically—all those who oppressed the 99 percent: police, bankers, landlords, employers, universities, politicians, the media, and the military. In response, the powers that be began a coordinated campaign to slander and suppress what had the potential to disrupt both production and commerce. Ultimately, OWS encampments were closed, mainly by police force, but OWS-inspired struggles live on, and the memory of what happened is very much alive.

Critics of OWS and "We are the 99 percent" say that the slogan is inaccurate. I disagree. It is true that there are well-to-do people in the 99 percent, and there are many in the 1 percent who are not that rich. The cutoff yearly household income for the 1 percent varies, ranging from $380,000 using the Census definition of income to nearly double that using that of the Federal Reserve, which includes capital gains. In some parts of the country, $380,000 would qualify a household as rich, while in others it would not. The flip side of this is that there are many people in the 99 percent who are not poor. There is a big difference between an income of $379,000 (just below the Census 1 percent cutoff) and $20,000, the cutoff for the poorest 20 percent of households.

We could argue as well that using income to divide the 99 percent and the 1 percent is inaccurate because what matters most is wealth. Ownership of stocks, bonds, real estate, unincorporated businesses, and the like is much more skewed than income, and it is at the top of the wealth distribution that economic and political power reside. The richest 1 percent of households now own an astonishing 42.4 percent of net financial assets (these exclude homes and mortgage debt).

But these arguments about the accuracy of the slogan miss the point. "We are the 99 percent" suggests an "us versus them" politics that foreshadows the class perspective so badly needed in the United States. Those who feel unfairly maligned because, although their incomes are high they are not rich, are free to ally themselves with their poorer brethren. And those who are objectively poor are done no harm by being lumped together with those whose incomes are higher. What the slogan does is help nurture a worldview that understands that not only is inequality out of control but that the position of the 1 percent comes at the expense of the rest of us. To invert and paraphrase the words of Bartolomeo Vanzetti, "their triumph is our agony." We can build upon this to create a politics that transcends the populism that passes for radicalism in the United States.

The issue here is not the literal meaning of the "1 percent," but power. Whether we speak of income or wealth, power resides in the households of the 1 percent. They own our workplaces and control our labor. They construct nearly every aspect of society—government, media, schools, culture—to maintain and increase their dominance over us. What the slogan, "We are the 99 percent," has done is bring power into the open and help change the political landscape.

Another criticism of "We are the 99 percent" argues that it implies a liberal politics of income redistribution and not a critique of capitalism. However, this ignores how OWS took shape. Public spaces were occupied; clashes with police ensued immediately; diverse discussions and debates took place; the movement spread rapidly across the nation and then the world; and millions of people were energized and made to feel part of something of great importance. Open air classrooms scrutinized critical issues. People learned that they could make decisions and effectively organize daily life. Those camped out in Zuccotti secured food and shelter, took care of sanitation, and solved complex problems of logistics every day.

These actions, combined with the anarchist and youthful sensibility and leadership of so much of OWS, gave rise to the posing of fundamental questions. What is democracy? Why don't we have it? How do we dispense with ubiquitous hierarchies? Why is there so little solidarity, compassion, love? Why aren't there enough jobs? Why is work so meaningless? Why do we devote so much of our lives to it? Why are we obsessed with making money and consuming things? Why are we destroying the environment that sustains us? Why does our government wage war against ordinary people, the 99 percent, all over the globe?

These questions cannot be answered, nor the issues they raise resolved, by more progressive taxes or a few expanded social welfare programs.

Our collective future is grim. Under our current political economic system, none of our major problems can be solved. Insecurity, inequality, and environmental destruction will get worse unless we take radical actions, repeatedly, for as long as necessary. OWS and "We are the 99 percent" were, and continue to be, ingenious interventions in what promises to be an era of growing class struggles. Other slogans will supplement "We are the 99 percent," but I hope that the idea that "we are the many, they are the few" remains foremost in our minds as we combat our class enemies.

11

THE GROWING
DEGRADATION OF WORK
AND LIFE AND WHAT WE
MIGHT DO TO END IT

One important reason why inequality has risen is that employer power has expanded enormously. Unions have crumbled and no longer offer much resistance to capital's rising strength. The rich have succeeded in shaping public policy in ways that greatly enhance their control of the economy. They can move their enterprises abroad or utilize cheap labor in other countries to do distance work, such as servicing customers online or doing programming and other labor for U.S. corporations. Their expansion to the rest of the world has forced peasants from their land and sped up movement of desperate people to the rich nations, where they provide a pool of cheap labor. In every workplace, employers utilize technology, such as robots and sophisticated logistics programs, as well as old-fashioned speed-ups, to economize on the use of labor, getting more output from ever fewer employees. Employees are expected to be at management's beck and call. The latter have even declared a war on sleep.[1] Saddled with debt, fearful of being fired, worried that a new job would be hard to find or worse than the one they just left, workers found it difficult to resist what was happening to them. The result has been a continuous decline in real wages for those with a high school education or less, those who once could earn a decent living in union manufacturing plants.

The median earnings of working men aged 30 to 45 without a high school diploma fell 20 percent from 1990 to 2013 when adjusted for inflation . . . Men with a high school diploma did only a little better, with a 13 percent decline in median earnings over the same span. Women did better than men, but it has been no era of riches for less-educated women either; those without a high school diploma saw a 12 percent decline in median earnings, and those with a high school diploma, or some college, a 3 percent gain.[2]

Karl Marx wrote of poles of wealth and misery. These have returned with a vengeance.[3]

In a recent *New York Times* article, former labor editor Steven Greenhouse writes about how employers in the service sector often demand that their employees work shifts that allow them little time for rest.[4] For example, a worker might have to close a night shift on Wednesday and open the morning shift on Thursday: "At Hudson County Community College in Jersey City, Ramsey Montanez struggles to stay alert on the mornings that he returns to his security guard station at 7 a.m., after wrapping up a 16-hour double shift at 11 p.m. the night before."[5] Given that it takes precious minutes to get home, at least an hour or two to wind down and take care of chores, and an hour or more to prepare and then get back to work next morning, Mr. Montanez probably has to get by on no more than five hours of sleep. If he has children or is responsible for the care of others, then the time crunch is still worse.

The practice of having employees close late and open early has become common enough that there is now a word for it—"clopening." Management justifies the practice by claiming that turnover in restaurant and other service jobs is so high that only the relatively few longer-term employees are sufficiently trustworthy and "have the authority and experience to close at night and open in the morning."[6] Labor advocates say that the reason for clopening is that scheduling is often no longer done by actual managers but by "sophisticated software"[7] purchased by companies.

Neither of these explanations suffice. The first implies that the fault lies with workers. However, turnover could be reduced by improved wages, hours, and working conditions.[8] That these have not been bettered suggests that turnover works to the advantage of service sector businesses. When shifts consist of people who have been on the job for many years, their loyalty to one another might come to outstrip their corporate fidelity, making them more willing to act collectively in opposition to their supervisors. They are more likely to insist on better treatment and to organize a union when demands are not met.

The second justification suggests that scheduling software is bought to lessen the burden of those who previously had to make work timetables. On the contrary, this software is used by corporations to squeeze as much work out of their employees as possible. The goal is to minimize unit labor costs and to achieve maximum control over the labor process, which encompasses every aspect of how work is performed.[9] Workers are conceptualized as mechanical cogs in a system that transforms inputs into outputs, and a host of managerial control techniques are implemented to force those hired to perform what they are ordered to do in a machine-like fashion.

An important modern control device is just-in-time inventory, meaning that a business keeps only as much inventory—car seats in an auto plant, frozen French fries in a fast-food restaurant—as will be needed over a very short period of time. This saves money on storage space and storage labor. In combination with other practices such as constantly shortening task times and using work teams in which members will pressure one another to solve production bottlenecks, it can help a business shave a few seconds from any particular assignment, whether it be moving a car along an assembly line or making a Big Mac.

However, today, just-in-time inventory is applied to workers themselves. Rather than assuming the utilization of someone for a week or even a day, scheduling is based upon an analysis of how many total work hours are likely to be needed during any particular hour or set of hours during a shift. If the scheduling program tells you that for an eight-hour shift, seven workers are needed for the first three and the last three hours but ten are needed for the two-hour period around lunchtime, then you will use ten workers only for those two hours. Employees may be scheduled for two-hour workdays or "on-call" personnel may be asked to come in.

One reason for the slow recovery of employment in the United States is the rising exploitation of those working. Corporations have used all of the control mechanisms at hand, techniques that have become both more sophisticated and punishing, to get fewer workers to convert ever more of their labor power into actual effort. This is true not just for manufacturing concerns like auto companies, which pioneered modern Taylorism, but by all private businesses (and public sector establishments such as colleges and the Social Security Administration), including especially today those in the service sector. Some have called the new forms of control, "management by stress," meaning that employers constantly stress the labor process to force more production out of less labor.[10] In economic terms, every second counts and eliminating a fraction of a second from the performance of a particular job detail means a great deal of money when applied to tens of millions of repetitions.[11] So, speed up the assembly line—and keep inventory, including labor, low. Reduce the size of work teams—but keep raising the output quota, outsource work to lower-wage countries, and super-exploit undocumented immigrants. Threaten those who can't keep up with demotion or firing, engage in constant electronic monitoring of employees on the job, even, as Henry Ford once did, keep tabs on the worker's private lives, which today often means eavesdropping on their Facebook and Twitter posts.[12]

From the workers' perspective, this pressure has consequences deleterious to mental and physical health. In the case of "clopening"— and other rest-depriving features of contemporary workplaces, such as compulsory overtime, split shifts, ten- and twelve-hour shifts, and inadequate break times—health problems such as high blood pressure, diabetes, and obesity often follow. Further, accidents and potentially deadly errors of omission are more likely at work, on the highways, and in the home. "According to the Institutes of Medicine, over one million injuries and between 50,000 and 100,000 deaths each year result from preventable medical errors, and many of these may be the result of insufficient sleep."[13]

Without adequate sleep, our mental functions are impaired, making it more difficult to comprehend what we are reading or what others are saying. We have little time and energy for meaningful social interactions, and as a consequence, family life can break down and we are discouraged from developing political awareness and participating in groups that benefit workers, such as labor unions and campaigns to improve wages, hours, and conditions of employment, the very things that could stop or radically diminish on-the-job stress.

When we combine relentless time pressure with the mind-numbing and physically destructive nature of most jobs, we have a recipe for acute human misery. There are millions of people toiling in office cubicles, call centers, daycare facilities, nursing homes, vegetable fields and orchards, automobile assembly lines and chicken, beef, and pork processing plants. Millions more work as retail clerks, hotel room attendants, adjunct professors, nannies, cooks, chauffeurs, lawn care workers, non-union and often immigrant construction workers, plumbers, electricians, dry wallers, homemakers. Every one of these jobs is stressful and poorly paid; none is secure, and none is immune from constant pervasive and dehumanizing managerial control.

What are some potential remedies? A few unions have clauses that compel minimum hours between shifts. Several others have been agitating for staffing levels that reduce fatigue and long hours, including the United Steel Workers in their recent strike against U.S. oil refineries.[14] However, unions cannot effectively combat "management by stress," in all of its dimensions, until they abandon the labor-management cooperation strategy that still has a stranglehold on them. Rather than confront employers, cooperating unions like the United Autoworkers have large cadres of union staff persons who actually help the companies stress the workers.[15]

A second line of attack is legislative. For "clopening," a model might be the European Union, which has established "a minimum daily rest period of 11 consecutive hours per 24-hour period."[16] But with union density in the United States as low as it was one hundred years ago, labor will have a difficult time getting states to enact a similar law, especially with its general unwillingness to politically mobilize members to confront legislators. (A good example is the "Wisconsin Uprising" of 2011. Nearly all national and state labor leaders quickly distanced themselves from the mass protests and retreated back into electoral politics, with disastrous results.)[17] Three states have introduced such a statute, but none has actually enacted one. And "clopening" is just one of many workplace stressors that make employees miserable.

Employers have their own solution. Do nothing. They argue that businesses will voluntarily address workplace problems when the market sends them signals that this is what employees want. This sounds ridiculous, but mainstream economists teach the (il)logic behind this to their students. Workers are assumed to be willing to pay for "good" jobs, which presumably would be those with reasonable scheduling, hours, and the like. The demand for such jobs would rise, and the "price" of them would increase. Here however, price means what employees are willing to pay for good jobs, in other words, what reduction in wages they would accept to have one. The reduction in wages would force employers to provide more such employment, because increasing the supply would raise their profits. By the same reasoning, wages are already factored into the disamenities of "bad" jobs, so, for example, those who "clopen" are already being rewarded for doing so.[18] I can't take the time here to show all of the things that are wrong with this analysis. Let's just say that in an economy with an enormous surplus of potential workers—nearly 18 million unemployed and underemployed as of January 2015, for a rate of 13.3 percent—those who own and manage businesses offer the choices to those they employ and not the other way round.[19]

What, then, might stem the tide of deteriorating workplace conditions? The typical strategy coming from progressives is market regulation. This is envisioned as a combination of labor union organization and agitation and political initiatives. In both cases, labor and other markets are taken as given (inevitable) and the only possibility is to set certain parameters, or limits, as to what market results are allowed to prevail. Unions can establish maximum hours per day or week, mandate rest periods, set wage rates, and so forth through collective bargaining. The state can be prevailed upon to do similar things for all workers, not just those in unions.

This strategy has had some success in the past, but today it hasn't yielded much for wage laborers. The working class struggled militantly for the eight-hour day in the 1880s, and after the Second World War, the eight-hour day became the norm for millions of workers, as did union-won vacations and holidays. Labor's power made alliances with other liberal groups possible and fruitful, especially in terms of the enactment of legislation beneficial to working men and women. Civil rights laws were passed; social security was expanded to include medical care and benefits increased substantially; workplace health and safety laws were ratified; the minimum wage rose significantly; public employee labor laws helped spur unionization; public housing was built; and affordable higher education, financed in part by the federal government, opened colleges and universities to the children of the working class.

Unfortunately, all of these gains have steadily eroded as employers regained the initiative in the mid-1970s and launched the ferocious neoliberal austerity that has dominated the United States ever since. Unions were caught unprepared and responded in a defeatist, defensive way, while their liberal allies deserted them. Labor leaders began to give employees dramatic concessions, and today givebacks have become so prevalent that it is an open question why a rational person would join a union. Strikes are remembered today mainly by retirees.[20] Nothing much can be expected of government, where the level of corruption is so great and the hold of our corporate overlords so strong that we believe we have achieved a remarkable victory when the government doesn't take something away from us.

Over the past 40 years, our expectations for a better economic future have steadily diminished. When Wal Mart agreed to raise its base wage to $10 an hour, one would have thought from the liberal and labor media that an incredible victory had been won. We seem to have forgotten that the federal minimum wage was worth more than this in terms of purchasing power in 1968. And the question is, what reason is there to imagine that in a global and neoliberal capitalism, matters won't continue to get worse into the indefinite future? Employers are relentless in their pursuit of profits, and they will always try, usually with success, to undermine whatever victories workers have achieved. Their single-minded focus on what Japanese car companies call "kaizen," or constant improvement, guarantees that the stress imposed upon those who toil for wages will never end. The global glut of potential laborers, which is part and parcel of the nature of our economic system, is never going to go away either, and it is this that makes managerial control possible in the first place.

The unhappy truth is that we can never beat at their own game those who own the world's capital. They rule the marketplace, and we do not; the government of almost every nation exists to aid and abet them; and the control over the billions of propertyless people in the world grows and deepens every day. Organizing within this hegemonic system while assuming that the market mechanism is inescapable, and being grateful for a few crumbs from its table, is a strategy guaranteed to fail.

The market is nothing more than a surface phenomenon, behind which lies the critical social relationship of unequal power, which means that focusing our efforts solely on regulation of the market ignores what is fundamental. So perhaps instead, we should make demands and take actions that threaten the market, that is, by directly attacking the power of those who are its masters and not accepting arrangements that allow the system to absorb our efforts and continue much as before. In addition, because the market is enveloped by an array of institutions—the state, media, schools—that buttress the power of those who control it, efforts to radically alter society must aim to change these as well.

How might we begin to do this? Initially, we could get as many organizations and individuals as possible to sign onto a list of general principles, formulated as a set of demands and commitments. The demands might include much shorter working hours, early and secure retirement, free universal healthcare, an end to the link between work and income, an end to all corporate subsidies, the immediate termination of all forms of discrimination, bans on fracking and other profit-driven environmental despoliations, an end to the war on terror and the closing of U.S. military bases in other countries, the abolition of the prison system, free schooling at all levels, open borders combined with the termination of U.S. financial support for oppressive governments, community-based policing, and the transfer of abandoned buildings and land to communities and groups who will put them to socially useful purposes. The commitments could embrace as many forms of collective self-help as imaginable (Cuban-style urban organic farming, cooperatives dedicated to education, child care, health, food provision, the establishment of worker-controlled enterprises), a shedding of excessive unnecessary possessions, a willingness to offer material support to local struggles aimed at empowering those without voice, a refusal to join the military or participate in the mindless and dangerous patriotism so prevalent in the United States, and a promise to educate ourselves and others about the nature of the system in whatever venues present themselves to us.

Four ancillary ideas flow from the establishment of principles and commitments. First, the details of these will naturally flow out of the specifics of actual events and struggles around them. For example, any efforts to end clopening could be tied directly to the need for shorter hours and more free time, which, in turn, could allow us to pose the question of why employers have the power to determine how we labor and with what intensity. Irregular and stressful shift work could even be connected to U.S. imperialism, which helps global corporations dispossess peasants in poor countries, forcing them unwillingly to migrate to rich nations where they intensify labor market competition and increase capital's power.

Second, whatever relatively small or local changes we fight for should always be connected to the larger and more global principles. Suppose that a coalition of progressive organizations seeks to end city tax subsidies to the builders of luxury condominiums. Why not tie this endeavor to demands for quality, low rent public housing, the considerable destruction of which has been caused by the luxury consumption of the wealthy, and our commitment to limit our own discretionary consumption?

Third, commitments should be part of a social process, in which we pledge ourselves to come to the aid of others. In New York City, a labor center named the Chinese Staff and Workers' Association helps employees who have suffered employer abuse, including unpaid wages. However, an aggrieved worker must agree to become part of the organization and help others facing similar problems. This builds the solidarity without which no change will occur, and it also helps members understand the collective nature of their oppression. Every organization like this one—and there should be thousands more, in every town and city—should demand commitment, so that we see that the troubles faced by others are ours as well.

Fourth, democratic, critical education is essential in all battles for radical social reconstruction. Such education should uncover the relevant facts and also delve deeply into the root causes of the problem at hand. It should conceive every political struggle as an opportunity to change the way we think about our lives and our connections to one another and the larger society. Or, as Henry Giroux said, we must "take seriously the issues of belief and persuasion, and once again give primacy to the symbolic and pedagogical dimensions of struggle as crucial weapons in the fight against neoliberalism and global capitalism."[21] Every organization must encourage and provide such education, seeing it as an integral part of a democratic and liberating politics.[22]

The philosopher Hegel said that "the truth is whole." The social phenomena that make up capitalist society are all interconnected, both cause and effect of one another. The demands and commitments we choose should encompass what we think are the most important elements of our society. As we act on these in a critical way, our grasp of the multitude of complex interrelationships is bound to deepen and strengthen our movements.

We live in an age of disposability. The drive to make money has now engulfed every part of the world and every aspect of our lives. This has been made possible in large part because movements to counter capital's power have either disappeared or seen their capacity to resist gravely weakened. Worse, to a considerable degree, this enfeebled ability to contest capital's strength has been self-inflicted. Labor unions and most organizations that claim to be progressive have no statements of principles, that is, to what they are committed and to what they are unalterably opposed. They hesitate to make radical demands, usually with the argument that such demands are utopian or that the time is not right. There is always an excuse.

The result has been a startling rise in inequality, with income and wealth accumulating at the top and the dominance of those who control the economy's commanding heights increasing, seemingly without limits. Capitalists now brook no compromises and make no concessions to any who would challenge their right to accumulate riches. No sense of obligation by the wealthy to society as a whole or to the mass of people without much income and wealth, much less a social contract between the rich and the rest of us, now exists or can even be imagined. Now, everyone is disposable; all of us are to be chewed up and spit out, used up until we are no longer useful as laborers to be exploited and as consumers to be shorn of our spending money. And some—black Americans, for example—have become especially disposable, often denied employment altogether, disproportionately harassed and shot by police, and pushed along a fast track to prison. This means that life has rapidly become more precarious, filled with fear and anxiety, as we wonder when we will be dumped in the trashcan, when those who wield unchallenged authority will dispose of us.

The administrators at the college where I taught used to tell us to tighten our belts this year so we could fight better next year. Yet all that happened was that we kept getting thinner. And pretty soon our laboring lives were over. Then the next generation was urged to do the same. Isn't it time for us to become protagonists, go on the offensive, attack our enemies head-on, study and learn from both successes and failures, always look for how things are connected, and see what happens? We don't have that much to lose.

Notes

1   https://adbusters.org/blogs/sleep-enemy.html
2   http://nytimes.com/2015/04/22/upshot/why-workers-without-much-education-are-being-hammered.html?_r=0&abt=0002&abg=1
3   http://business.time.com/2013/03/25/marxs-revenge-how-class-struggle-is-shaping-the-world/
4   http://nytimes.com/2015/02/22/business/late-to-bed-early-to-rise-and-working-tired.html?_r=1

5   Ibid.
6   Ibid.
7   Ibid.
8   http://cepr.net/documents/publications/min-wage-2013-02.pdf
9   See Harry Braverman, Labor and Monopoly Capital: The Degradation of Work in the Twentieth Century, 25th Anniversary Edition (New York: Monthly Review Press, 1998).
10 See Jane Slaughter, "Management by Stress," Multinational Monitor, Vol. 11, Nos. 12 and 2 (January/February, 1990), http://multinationalmonitor.org/hyper/issues/1990/01/slaughter.html. Also, Mike Parker and Jane Slaughter, Choosing Sides: Unions and the Team Concept (Boston: South End Press, 1988) and Karl Taro Greenfeld, "Taco Bell and the Golden Age of Drive-Thru," Bloomberg Business, May 5, 2011. http://bloomberg.com/bw/magazine/content/11_20/b4228064581642.htm
11 Kim Moody, Workers in a Lean World: Unions in the International Economy (London: Verso, 1997); Kim Moody, US Labor in Trouble and Transition: The Failure of Reform From Above, the Promise of Revival from Below (London: Verso, 2007).
12 http://scholarship.law.duke.edu/cgi/viewcontent.cgi?article=3255&context=dlj
13 http://healthysleep.med.harvard.edu/healthy/matters/consequences/sleep-performance-and-public-safety
14 http://mrzine.monthlyreview.org/2015/early040215.html
15 See Gregg Shotwell, Autoworkers Under the Gun: A Shop-Floor View of the End of the American Dream (Chicago: Haymarket, 2012).
16 Greenhouse, "In Service Sector, No Rest for the Working."
17 See the essays in Michael D. Yates, editor, Wisconsin Uprising: Labor Fights Back (New York: Monthly Review Press, 2011).
18 See Michael D. Yates, Naming the System: Inequality and Work in the Global Economy (New York: Monthly Review Press, 2003), chapter 5 ("The Neoclassical/ Neoliberal Dogma").
19 http://bls.gov/news.release/empsit.nr0.htm; http://bls.gov/news.release/empsit.t15.htm
20 http://bls.gov/news.release/wkstp.t01.htm
21 Henry Giroux, personal correspondence.
22 The most insightful modern thinker on critical pedagogy is Henry Giroux. For many easy to access essays by him, see http://truth-out.org. An excellent recent article by him is "Higher Education and the Promise of Insurgent Public Memory," http://truth-out.org/news/item/29396-higher-education-and-the-promise-of-insurgent-public-memory

12
GLOBAL INEQUALITY

The previous chapters dealt mainly with inequality in the United States. What is true there is also the case for much of the world. Many of the reasons for this are similar to those for the United States. However, each nation has its own history, and there are significant differences between the United States and other countries. Following the procedure used in the rest of this book, we will look first at the data on global inequality and then look at some of its implications.

If we look at inequality within individual countries, we see that it has risen in most of them, a fact that the business-oriented World Economic Forum identifies in a survey as an extremely pressing global issue, one that is "impacting social stability within countries and threatening security on a global scale."[1] Given the statistics, this is not surprising, although the reference to global security expresses mainly the fears of the elite and has little to do with the conditions of those who keep falling farther behind those at the top.

One way to see the increase in inequality around the globe is to look at the Gini Coefficient, a concept introduced in Chapter 2. Remember that this indicator has a value of 0 if there is perfect equality in income or wealth. That is, each one-fifth of the population (the poorest, second, middle, fourth, and richest quintiles) receive exactly 20 percent of total income or wealth. Figure 12.1 shows this coefficient (for income) for most of the world's rich nations, as well as a few other poor and rapidly growing economies outside of Europe and North America.[2] Notice that the coefficient for the United States is exceeded only by that for Turkey, Mexico, Chile, Indonesia, Argentina, China, Latvia, Brazil, Colombia, and South Africa.

These numbers don't tell us whether income inequality has been increasing or decreasing. We know that it has increased dramatically in the United States, but what about the rest of the world? Our knowledge here is inexact, because there are many nations, especially very poor ones, in which data collection is either sparse or nonexistent. Casual observations seem to show that there is hardly a place on the globe today where the very rich do not dominate social, political, and economic life and where those without means have not been suffering a worsening litany of woes, from dire poverty and underemployment to wars, hunger, and disease. So, it is probably a safe bet to say that, in those countries where decent data are not available, inequality has grown. We do have good data for many of the countries listed in Figure 12.1. Figures 12.2 and 12.3 reveal that income inequality has indeed grown in most of the rich nations.[3] Observe that the Scandinavian nations, long noted for their relatively low levels of inequality, show considerable increases since 1980, over the period when neoliberal capitalism took firm hold of the world's economies.

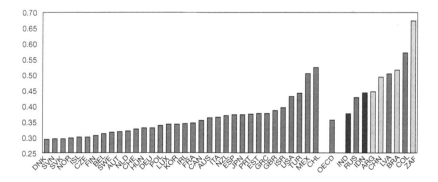

Figure 12.1 Gini Coefficients for Select Countries

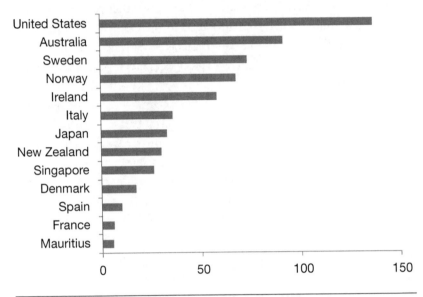

Figure 12.2 Increase in Income Share of the Top 1 Percent Since 1980

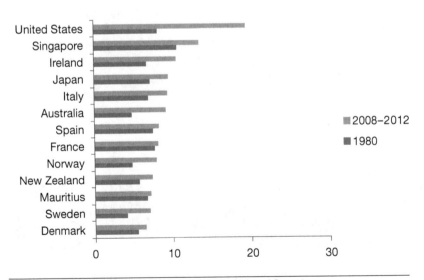

■ 2008–2012
■ 1980

Figure 12.3 The Share of National Income Going to the Richest 1 Percent

Throughout the world, wealth is distributed much more unequally than income. In its 2014 survey of global wealth, Credit Suisse lays out the basic facts:

> In almost all countries, the mean wealth of the top decile (i.e. the wealthiest 10% of adults) is more than ten times median wealth. For the top percentile (i.e. the wealthiest 1% of adults), mean wealth exceeds 100 times median wealth in many countries and can approach 1000 times the median in the most unequal nations. This has been the case throughout most of human history, with wealth ownership often equating with land holdings, and wealth more often acquired via inheritance or conquest rather than talent or hard work.[4]

For a variety of reasons—world wars, revolutions, the strength of left-wing political movements, wealth taxation—the distribution of wealth became more equal throughout most of the twentieth century. However, and especially since the financial meltdown that triggered the worldwide Great Recession in 2007, wealth inequality has begun to rise. In terms of current wealth inequality, Credit Suisse has developed a ranking scheme based on the share of wealth held by the richest 10 percent of individuals in a given country. Table 12.1 shows the results.[5]

Trends in wealth inequality vary, but since the Great Recession, they have shown more increases than decreases in the world's nations. One of Thomas Piketty's major predictions in his monumental *Capital in the Twenty-First Century* is that wealth concentration is likely to rise and approach that existing before the First World War initiated a long period of wealth destruction, expropriation, and taxation, all of which greatly reduced inequality. Two forces are now at work to reverse this long-term movement. First, most capitalist economies are experiencing and are likely to continue to face low output and income growth, as the forces generating high growth, such as employment-generating technological change, intense market competition, and high government spending, peter out. Low growth limits the likelihood of new groups and individuals accumulating wealth, leaving the field to those who already have

Table 12.1 Wealth Inequality, 2014

	Developed Economies		Emerging Markets	
Very high inequality top decile share > 70% (USA c1910)	Hong Kong Switzerland United States		Argentina Brazil Egypt India Indonesia Malaysia	Peru Philippines Russia South Africa Thailand Turkey
High inequality top decile share > 60% (e.g. USA c1950)	Austria Denmark Germany	Israel Norway Sweden	Chile China Columbia Czech Republic Korea	Mexico Poland Saudi Arabia Taiwan
Medium inequality top decile share > 50% (e.g. Europe c1980)	Australia Canada Finland France Greece Ireland Italy	Netherlands New Zealand Portugal Singapore Spain United Kingdom	United Arab Emirates	
Low inequality top decile share < 50%	Belgium Japan			

done so. The latter then will leave their assets to heirs, limiting the dilution of national wealth. Second, the rate of return on capital, especially the financial assets that comprise disproportionally large shares of the riches of the highest income recipients, has been and will continue to be higher than the rate of growth of economies. This has much to do with the opening up of global markets to financial asset speculation and the seemingly endless capacity of titans of finance like George Soros to engage in various kinds of arbitrage (finding small discrepancies in what an asset should sell for and what it is in fact selling for) to accumulate enormous sums of money in short periods of time.[6]

Credit Suisse finds some evidence for Piketty's predictions. Between 2000 and 2014, the following countries saw increases in either the share of the wealthiest 10 percent, 1 percent, or both: Argentina, Austria,

Chile, China, Czech Republic, Egypt, Greece, Hong Kong, India, Indonesia, Ireland, Russia, South Korea, Spain, Taiwan, Turkey, United Arab Emirates, and United Kingdom. If 2007 had been used instead of 2000, many more nations would be added to this list. And in either case, few places showed declines in wealth inequality; the best that could be said for those that did not exhibit an increase is that the wealth gap between the top and everyone else remained flat.

Piketty's perspective is considerably more long-term than fourteen years. His approach is to calculate the ratio of national wealth to national income, to ask how many years of a country's total income it would take to equal total wealth. Because wealth represents ownership of assets and is not in itself productive, whereas income represents output actually produced in the current year, this ratio represents the weight of ownership to present economic activity. In dynamic capitalist economies, with active governments that do not unduly reward ownership per se, this ratio will tend to fall. Piketty shows that over most of the twentieth century, it did fall in all rich capitalist countries. However, beginning roughly in the 1970s, this decline has been reversed. For the two reasons noted above, Piketty thinks that this ratio will continue to rise, meaning that inequality will worsen, approaching that existing before the First World War. Those who are extraordinarily wealthy will leave their assets to their children, assets that will continue to grow in money value irrespective of the social productiveness of their owners. Societies will be thoroughly dominated by those with the most wealth, and democracy will become more and more a dead letter. If we were to examine a random selection of, say, twenty capitalist nations, subjecting them to what I have subjected the United States in this book, we would find more similarities than differences.

Looking at different nations and determining the extent of and trend in inequality is not what is usually meant by global inequality. As former World Bank economist and pioneer in the study of global inequality, Branko Milanovic, tells us, there are three ways to describe economic disparities worldwide.[7] First, we can examine inequality among countries, without reference to individual, household, or family incomes and wealth. This is typically done by finding mean incomes for each country (total national income divided by the number of people) and then calculating a Gini Coefficient (GC) for these mean incomes. Typically, we are interested in whether or not the national incomes of richer nations are diverging or converging from those of poorer countries.

This is of interest because of how capitalism began and developed. From its origins in England and Western Europe, capitalism spread, by means of violence—conquest, mass murder, colonization, the slave trade—to embrace most of the world. It left in its wake two types of economies, a few rich and many poor. It is remarkable how stable this typology has remained, with a few later additions to the rich countries, over nearly 300 years. At the top in terms of per capita income and wealth stand the nations of Western Europe, the Scandinavian countries, the United States, Australia, New Zealand, and Japan, and perhaps South Korea, Taiwan, and a few others. Moving toward becoming rich capitalist countries might be China, Brazil, India, and Russia, though it is by no means certain that they will achieve this status. The rest of the world is mired in multiple kinds of wretchedness, though most have a small stratum of high income and wealthy individuals. As with the ability of the economic elite to secure fortunes across many generations, so too those countries that developed first have been able to maintain their global dominance.

Solid evidence buttresses the preceding sentence. World Bank economist Lant Pritchett found that the gap between the richest capitalist nation, the United States, and the world's poorest states rose dramatically between 1870 and 1960, from a per capita income ratio of about nine in the former year to more than fifty in the latter.[8] A few poor nations did achieve per capita income growth rates higher than those in the rich nations; that is, they were converging rather than diverging. Pritchett asked how long it would take for these countries to become equal to the rich ones. Here is what he said about India:

> a few developing countries were actually converging, that is, they were growing faster than the United States. When are these lucky convergers going to overtake the United States? India, for example, registered an annual average growth rate of 3 percent between 1980

and 1993. If India could sustain this pace for another 100 years, its income would reach the level of high-income countries today. And, if India can sustain this growth differential for 377 years, my great-great-great-great-great-great-great-great-great-great-great-grandchildren will be alive to see India's income level converge.[9]

Given that no capitalist economy, nor indeed the global capitalist economy, has grown at anywhere near a rate of 3 percent per year for 100 years, much less 377, this seems unlikely indeed. Even China, with its astonishing recent growth rates, will not be able to sustain such a rate for more than a century.

Pritchett's study noted divergence between 1870 and 1960. What happened after this? Milanovic shows that global inequality according to this first concept was roughly constant between 1960 and 1980, rose dramatically from 1980 until 2000, fell until the beginning of recovery after the Great Recession, and then began to rise again. Irrespective of the fall in the 2000s, inequality among nations is still extremely high, much higher than in 1960. No real convergence has taken place.

The second method of calculating global inequality takes cognizance of the fact that nations have widely different populations. With the first technique, each country has equal weight, the least populated the same as the most. With the second, national income is weighted by each country's population, which means, for example, that a rising per capita income in China counts for much more than a similar increase is Tanzania. If we do this and then ask if there is divergence or convergence, we get a slight convergence between rich and poor nations from 1950 until 1990. However, after 1990, there is a sharp convergence. While most poor countries are not converging, the two largest ones, China and India, are. Incomes for hundreds of millions of Chinese and Indians have risen dramatically, and because these nations have a combined population of 2.7 billion—37.5 percent of the world's population—they count for much more than most nations in terms of national income. They alone account for the convergence shown by method 2. If we excluded them, there would be no convergence between rich and poor places.

It is interesting to note that, despite the fact that incomes have risen for many Indians and Chinese, inequality in both wealth and income have risen significantly in both countries. Furthermore, while money incomes are higher for peasants in China than they were before its leaders pushed it sharply toward capitalism, more than 600 million rural dwellers have lost their communal lands and their collectively provided food rations and medical care, none of which is subtracted from their current money incomes. Furthermore, the likelihood that either China or India will continue on a very high growth rate path is negligible. No society can suppress consumption indefinitely to finance capital spending, which is the engine of economic growth. Workers have to be exploited, reserves of labor have to be moved, by force or otherwise, from the countryside to urban areas, and the misery caused by these must certainly generate opposition, such as strikes, demonstrations, and violence. None of these acts of class struggle please global capital, which, if they happen often enough or if the ruling elites in India and China capitulate and allow wages and employment conditions to improve, will shift their capital elsewhere. This has already been happening in China as pressure from workers has forced up wages.[10] And even if we suppose that stratospheric growth can be sustained, it will soon enough generate environmental catastrophe. Already both nations foul the atmosphere and otherwise degrade Mother Earth to an unconscionable degree. China has made some efforts to moderate the despoliation of its air, water, and land, but not nearly enough to counter its insatiable demand for fossil fuels. India hasn't done much of anything.[11] All of this strongly suggests that economic equality among nations is a pipedream, and whatever convergence has taken place will not be lasting.

The third manner in which we can define and measure inequality is what Milanovich terms "true global inequality." Here, what is done within countries is done for the world. Household incomes or wealth are tabulated from a sample of household surveys in as many nations as possible, and then the usual division into quintiles, deciles, ventiles, and/or percentiles allows us to see trends in distribution. Such canvasing does not take place very often, and not at all before the late 1980s. Before this, some major countries did not do household surveys, and even today, there are nations, mainly among the poorest, that do not conduct them. Therefore, the data we have are recent, and they are not inclusive; we have to take them with a grain of salt. This is not to say that the data are wrong, only that the margin of error is larger than we might like it to be.

What do we see if we look at world inequality at the household level? To make comparisons across countries, household incomes have to be put on a common footing. This is done through the use of "purchasing power parity" (PPP) exchange rates. That is, we take a basket of goods and services and ask, what would the basket cost in each country? If, for example, it cost $1,000 in the United States and 60,000 rupees in India, the dollar–rupee exchange rate would be 60 rupees per dollar. A household in India with a yearly income of 1,000,000 rupees would have the same income as a U.S. household with a yearly income of $16,667 (one million divided by sixty). We could convert every household income in the world into dollars (or any other currency) in this way. Then we could rank the incomes from lowest to highest and construct a standard income distribution table, showing, for example, the share of global income received by the poorest 20 percent, the next poorest, the middle, the next richest, and the richest 20 percent. We could also measure the income share of the richest 5 and 1 percent, and so forth. A Gini Coefficient could easily be calculated.

Several interesting facts can be discerned from the data on global inequality. First, inequality in the world as a whole is greater than that within any one nation. The Gini Coefficient for the globe is about .7, which is .1 higher than in Brazil, one of the most unequal nations on earth. As great as income differences are in the United States, they are only about half as great as in the world. Second, as Milanovic asks, what exactly does a Gini Coefficient of .7 mean? He answers with two enlightening examples:

One way to look at it is to take the whole income of the world and divide it into two halves: the richest 8% will take one-half and the other 92% of the population will take another half. So, it is a 92–8 world. Applying the same type of division to the U.S. income, the numbers are 78 and 22. Or using Germany, the numbers are 71 and 29. Another way to look at it is to compare what percentage of world population, ranked from the poorest to the richest, is needed to get to the cumulative one-fifths of global income. Three-quarters of (the poorer) world population are needed to get to the first ⅕th of total income, but only 1.7% of those at the top suffice to get to the last one-fifth.[12]

Third, as of 2008, when the last surveys were taken, global inequality appears to have fallen slightly. If true, it has probably been due to a decline in the number of truly destitute persons, at least in terms of money income, in China and India.[13] However, this decrease must be seen against the astonishingly high level of income disparity from which this is measured. If I make a billion dollars a year, and you make $1,000, and then you see an increase of a few thousand dollars, you are closer to me, but so what? What real meaning, in terms of power, for example, can we attribute to this? "Nothing" is the obvious answer.

Fourth, the spread of market relationships over the past several decades has created economic winners and losers. Between 1988 and 2008, the global 1 percent have seen their incomes increase substantially and those between the 90th and 99th percentile saw moderate gains, while those in the bottom 5 percent faced stagnant incomes and fell further behind. Surprisingly, those between the 75th and 90th percentile did not gain and some actually lost income. Also of interest and importance is that the quarter of households above the bottom 5 percent gained income, as did what Milanovic calls the global middle class. Among the latter group are "some 200 million Chinese, 90 million Indians, and about 30 million people each from Indonesia, Brazil and Egypt."[14] Undoubtedly, the Great Recession and slow recovery has weakened income growth for all but the extremely wealthy. And this might have dampened the rising expectations of globalization's "winners." However, the global middle class adds a conservative element to politics that should not be overlooked. Those with a growing stake in maintaining their incomes and consumption are not all that likely to participate in efforts to bring about radical change. Even if we suppose that a dampening of expectations angers many in this group, the result might be a politics of resentment against those below them.

What can we surmise from this excursion into statistics? If we can say one thing for certain, it is that the world is structured economically and politically in an extremely unequal way. No matter where we look, whether in the rich capitalist nations, rapidly growing ones like China and India, or the poorest countries, the richest and wealthiest people take the lion's share of income and wealth, and most of the increases in these over the past forty years have accrued to them. Everywhere, this translates into disproportionate power in all spheres of life. What is more, although many millions of poor people are now a bit less unfortunate, there is no reason to think that sharp increases in equality are on either the immediate horizon or waiting to burst onto the scene at some distant date. Given this, without major oppositional efforts by working persons, peasants, the unemployed, and the dispossessed, the world is going to become increasingly undemocratic and oligarchic.

With respect to the forces responsible for inequality around the world, the one that stands out is the inability of working people and peasants to mount credible resistance. In the most advanced capitalist nations, labor union density has fallen, sometimes, as in the United States, precipitously. Unions and labor movements always have reduced inequality.[15] Their power in Western Europe and the Scandinavian countries is the main reason why these exhibit more income equality than almost any other region on earth. Yet, in these places, labor is getting steadily weaker, unable to counter the growing power of capital. With the demise of the Soviet Union, which served as an ideological counterweight to capitalist hegemony, employers and governments in Europe no longer need to cater to the needs of workers, lest the latter become more radical in their thoughts and actions.

Capital now moves freely across borders, seeking ever-cheaper labor, further lowering labor's power. In the poorer countries to which capital increasingly moves, notably China and India (but also Vietnam, Indonesia, and elsewhere in Asia) elites seek to keep wages low so that corporate profits are high and their share of them continues to rise. At the same time, tens of millions of peasants have been forced from their land, providing a ready reserve army of labor in towns and cities. States do whatever is necessary to maintain safe and prosperous havens for transnational companies, including extreme violence when necessary. They also employ time-honored tactics of divide and conquer, pitting one ethnic or religious group against another. Occasionally, governments even will allow for some minimal relief from the misery of the masses of workers and peasants, if only to coopt more aggressive antagonism from those who have lost income and wealth or those whose upward mobility seems permanently blocked. When those who toil for a living are quiescent, capital is given a free reign, and governments are more than willing to grant businesses and their wealthy owners every manner of concession, from tax exemptions to abolition or non-enforcement of environmental protections.

The world is awash in protest movements, all of which, it can be argued plausibly, have their roots in burgeoning inequality. Not necessarily in inequality per se, but in what has caused it. The Arab Spring in nations like Egypt was fueled by suppression of workers' rights, increases in the prices of necessities like bread, capital-friendly political leaders, an absence of democracy, theft of peasant lands, lack of employment opportunities, declining real wages, and so on. Workers in China have been striking and otherwise protesting in record numbers, stricken by long hours, low wages, unsafe workplaces, poor or no housing, unbreathable air, an autocratic government, and the seemingly unlimited wealth and power of their bosses. In India, peasants, under the banner of communist parties, have begun to wage guerilla war. In France, workers take to the streets every time the government seeks to lower their living standards. In the United States, as we have seen in previous chapters, many uprisings have taken place. The same is true in Canada. Pick a country, and you will see resistance.

Yet despite these efforts, victories have been fleeting. A military dictatorship once again rules Egypt. Bashar al-Assad continues his genocidal onslaught against the people of Syria. Civil war engulfs Ukraine. China's undemocratic and autocratic Communist Party is still firmly in control of Chinese politics and society. The Venezuelan government is trying valiantly to continue the Bolivarian Revolution begun by Hugo Chavez but falling oil prices and U.S. sabotage, which could well be connected, have put Venezuela's future as an important outpost of noncapitalist development in jeopardy. Throughout the world, protest has often enough devolved into ethnic and religious violence and warfare.

What then, might be done to counter inequality and put the world on a more peaceful and egalitarian path? Thomas Piketty and Branco Milanovic have suggestions, which on their face are unobjectionable. Piketty recommends a global progressive wealth tax, enforced by an agreement among nations. Funds from such a tax could be used to enact policies that greatly lessen the distance between richer and poorer. Milanovic says that global inequality can be attacked by rich countries transferring income to poorer nations, poor persons migrating to rich countries, and people fighting for greater inequality within nations. Piketty proposes that his tax be debated democratically and then enacted through political consensus. This seems extremely naïve, especially because the rapid growth of inequality has precluded democratic debate. Milanovic, on the other hand, is skeptical of the first two of his suggestions. Rich nations now give precious little aid to poor ones, and political realities make this unlikely to change. He appears to believe that mass outmigration by the poor to wealthy countries would greatly benefit the new immigrants. This is because, for example, the poorest 20 percent of Danish households have an average income equal to the 80 percentile of the world's households. He admits that today's political climates make this unrealistic. But even if there were large-scale migrations, the recent arrivals would swamp low-wage labor markets, lowering the wages of all poor workers, while the immigrants would suffer the worst kinds of exploitation, not a circumstance likely to advance their or their children's life prospects. Surely, we should be free to move to wherever we choose, and we should also have the right, as labor journalist, photographer, and activist, David Bacon argues, to stay home.[16] But neither will matter much, absent efforts to enforce these rights.

What needs to happen is resistance within every country and maximum solidarity among all workers and peasants, in rich and poor countries alike. The details of such struggles have to be worked out in each place, though there is no reason to believe that the propositions laid out in Chapter 11 wouldn't be useful and resonate around the world. The key is solidarity by all workers and peasants, within and between the states of the world. Milanovic thinks this especially unlikely; he has an interesting discussion of the data showing that most inequality now is due to that among countries rather than that between high and low income recipients (which he uses as a proxy for class inequality) within countries.[17] It is no longer useful to say, as Marx did in the *Manifesto of the Communist Party*, "Working Men of All Countries, Unite!" Workers in rich and poor countries face almost incomprehensibly different circumstances, unlike when Marx lived. So what exactly unites them? Here, Milanovic has a point, but he is wrong in three senses. First, solidarity is notoriously difficult to forge in any particular nation. Second, acts of international solidarity are not unique, as a perusal of *Labor Notes* and similar publications shows. Third, there really is no choice but for whatever ties bind us objectively to begin to bind us subjectively. We all want democracy. We are all exploited by our country's and the world's economic masters. We all want this to end, so that we might enjoy the fruits of our labor and happier, healthier lives. We all want healthcare, pensions, vacations, holidays, quality education, control over the labor we do, work that utilizes our full human capacities, societies in which children can grow up safe and sound, livable environments, an end to war and all other types of strife, and many others. There are still plenty of things to unite us.

Those of us in the rich capitalist nations have special responsibilities in all of this. It has been, after all, our countries that have immiserated the rest of the world. We need, first of all, to get our own houses in order, forging solidarity at home as we confront our employers and our governments to change their ways. We must do all we can to stop the imperialism that wreaks more havoc around the planet every day. Second, we need to join hands as often and in whatever ways possible with those suffering in other places, no matter how far away and no matter the issue. We must firmly reject the mindless nationalism that makes international cohesion so difficult.

So many awful events are happening now, in every corner of the globe, that it is difficult to maintain hope. Yet, without hope, we might as well give up altogether and let capitalism continue to generate maximum misery everywhere. We should be cognizant of the words of Emiliano Zapata and Antonio Gramsci. Zapata said that it is better to die on our feet than live on our knees. Gramsci implored us to have a pessimism of the intellect and an optimism of the will.

Notes

1 World Economic Forum, Outlook on the Global Agenda 2014, the 1980s.
2 Figure 12.1 is taken from OECD, In It Together: Why Less Inequality Benefits All (Paris: OECD Publishing, 2015), 6. The bar for OECD is an average for the 34 countries in the Organization for Economic Co-operation and Development. The OECD is an international organization established to foster trade and economic progress.
3 These two tables are taken from https://oxfam.org/sites/www.oxfam.org/files/bp-working-for-few-political-capture-economic-inequality-200114-summ-en.pdf. The original source for the tables is F. Alvaredo, A. B. Atkinson, T. Piketty, and E. Saez, "The World Top Incomes Database," 2013, http://topincomes.g-mond.parisschoolof economics.eu/. The second table only include countries with data in 1980 and later than 2008.
4 https://publications.credit-suisse.com/tasks/render/file/?fileID=5521F296-D460-2B88-081889DB12817E02
5 Ibid.
6 For a detailed review of Piketty's book, see John Bellamy Foster and Michael D. Yates, "Thomas Piketty and the Crisis of Neoclassical Economics," Monthly Review, 66/6 (November 2015).
7 Branko Milanovic, "Global Income Inequality by the Numbers: in History and Now," http://elibrary.worldbank.org/doi/pdf/10.1596/1813-9450-6259.
8 Pritchett's article, "Forget Convergence: Divergence Past, Present, and Future," can be found at https://imf.org/external/pubs/ft/fandd/1996/06/pdf/pritchet.pdf
9 Ibid.
10 http://economist.com/news/briefing/21646180-rising-chinese-wages-will-only-strengthen-asias-hold-manufacturing-tightening-grip
11 See Richard Smith, "China's Communist-Capitalist Ecological Apocalypse," http://truth-out.org/news/item/31478-china-s-communist-capitalist-ecological-apocalypse; http://nytimes.com/2013/03/30/world/asia/cost-of-environmental-degradation-in-china-is-growing.html?_r=0; http://theatlantic.com/international/archive/2012/02/india-is-burning-how-rapid-growth-is-destroying-its-environment-and-future/253214/; http://qz.com/307176/thirteen-of-the-20-most-polluted-cities-in-the-world-are-indian/
12 Milanovic, "Global Income Inequality by the Numbers: in History and Now."
13 Ibid.
14 Ibid.

15   Florence Jaumotte and Carolina Osorio Buitroni, "Power from the People," Finance
      & Development, 52, 1 (March 2015), http://imf.org/external/pubs/ft/fandd/2015/03/
      jaumotte.htm
16   David Bacon, The Right to Stay Home: How US Policy Drives Mexican Migration
      (Boston: Beacon Press, 2013).
17   Milanovic, "Global Income Inequality by the Numbers: in History and Now."

INDEX

Page numbers in *italics* refer to figures and tables.